Revival Fires

ANOINTED GENERALS
Past & Present

Part Two
of Four

By Dr. Alan Pateman

By Dr. Jennifer Pateman

Available from APMI Publications, Amazon.com and Other Retail Outlets

Revival Fires

ANOINTED
GENERALS
Past & Present

*Part Two
of Four*

DR. ALAN PATEMAN

BOOK TITLE:
Revival Fires, Anointed Generals Past and Present (Part Two of Four)

WRITTEN BY Dr. ALAN PATEMAN
ISBN: 978-1-909132-36-8
eBook ISBN: 978-1-909132-52-8

Published By:
APMI Publications
In Partnership with Truth for the Journey Books **10**
Email: publications@alanpateman.com
www.AlanPatemanMinistries.com

Acknowledgements:
Author/Design/Senior Editor/Publisher: Apostle Dr. Alan Pateman
Editing/Proofreading/Research: Dr. Jennifer Pateman
Computer Administration/Office Manager: Dr. Dorothea Struhlik

❖

Dedication

Special big thanks to my wonderful wife Jenny. She is a true intercessor and woman of God; she is truly bone of my bone and flesh of my flesh. For her practical help in guidance, typing and editing skills.

A ministry like this cannot exist without the practical support and the many prayers of those prayer warriors, which we call our partners. Partners thank you for your love and support, especially Dorothea Struhlik, my administrator who tirelessly works to fulfil the tasks in hand.

Finally, Peter and Muriel Johnston *(Jenny's Mum and Dad)* who have been diligent in their support. Pastors Tony and Josie Botfield of Oasis Christian Fellowship Telford UK for their on-going encouragement. You have really helped to make a difference. May God reward all of you, in His unlimited supply of unconditional and divine love.

❖

Acknowledgements

While many of us give our undivided attention to those who in our eyes are successful, to the so-called professionals, the famous, because of their books, television ministries, churches of thousands, crusades that reach the masses. These are of course, in the majority of cases the people whom we should look to, in the sense of them being anointed, faithful, obedient and therefore effective, which inspires us to success in our given quest.

These are the Pauls and perhaps likewise we are the Timothys. This material endeavours to enhance to the glory of God, their successes. However I desire right at the beginning of this book to give a tribute to the thousands/ millions of the unknowns in this world who are just as called, dedicated, sold out and anointed. People whom many children *(including us adults),* call Mom, Dad or Uncle!

To those who spend many hours in their closet, night after night praying for revival. For the very faithful who make the tea or clean the floor or drive the car to bring those that desire to the church meeting or the crusade and those who move the chairs or work behind the scenes, **to all such kind I give you a tribute and say,** *Thank You.*

For He above knows your faithfulness and at the right time you will reap your reward along with those others, your fellow co-workers whom you can read about in this book, *"Revival Fires - Anointed Generals, Past and Present" (Part Two of Four)*.

❖

Table of Contents

❖

Foreword

This is the time of new beginnings, perhaps some might say, *"Now is the count down for the Lord's return...,"* but the fact remains, there is much work to be done. We need stable, trained and Spirit led harvesters that are willing to go out into the harvest field.

Seasons might be changing but God's Word remains the same. The heart of the author is to help train, equip and be a blessing to those men and women who will be willing to fulfil their potential in ministry and be properly equipped for service. ***Desiring all believers to walk and live in the Authority and Power of God's Word and His Precious Holy Spirit.***

Below is a prophecy attributed to Smith Wigglesworth in 1947. I believe this is speaking of the time we are living in:

"During the next few decades there will be two distinct moves of the Holy Spirit across the Church in Great Britain.

- *The first move* will affect every church that is open to receive it, and will be characterized by a restoration of the baptism and gifts of the Holy Spirit.

- *The second move* of the Holy Spirit will result in people leaving historic churches and planting new churches. In the duration of each of these moves, the people who are involved will say, 'This is a great revival.' But the Lord says, 'No, neither is this the great revival but both are steps towards it.'

When the new Church phase is on the wane, there will be evidence in the churches of something that has not been seen before: *a coming together of those with an emphasis on the Word and those with an emphasis on the Spirit.* When the Word and the Spirit come together, there will be the biggest move of the Holy Spirit that the nation, and indeed, the world has ever seen.

This will mark the beginning of a revival that will eclipse anything that has been witnessed within these shores, even the Wesleyan and Welsh revivals of former years. The outpouring of God's Spirit will flow over from the United Kingdom to mainland Europe, and from there, will begin a missionary move to the ends of the earth."

Part One

THE PENTECOSTAL ORIGIN

❖

CHAPTER 1

Visitation in Wales

The great Welsh revival of 1904 started a year or two before the mighty out-pouring of God's Spirit at Azusa Street.

It is impossible, and would be historically incorrect, to dissociate the Pentecostal Movement from the remarkable visitation of God's Holy Spirit in Wales. The young Welshman in question, Evan Roberts, was born June 8, 1878, into the staunch Calvinist-Methodist home of Henry and Hannah Roberts, in the little Welsh town of Loughor, *(this is some eight miles from Swansea, the South of Wales).*

Evan, in common with many other boys in the Welsh valleys began work at an early age in a coalmine. When he was older he took up the trade of a blacksmith in connection with the mines. From his early teen years the hand of God rested upon him. Perhaps this was due to his parents who had a strong influence in cultivating that spirit and nature within him.

His nature was one of excellence and sensitivity. The family was known for their love of God's Word and hard work. Each family member, no matter how young, had his own well-worn bible. #1

> *"A revivalist spirit was built immediately within him."*
> *(Roberts Liardon)*

What would Jesus Do?

Evan was dramatically different from the rest of the boys his age. He never took part in sports, amusements, or coarse joking. He worked in the mines every day, then came home and walked a mile to his church, *Moriah Chapel.*

- At thirteen years of age, Evan vowed to commit himself even further to the work of the Lord.

- One simple yet profound phrase spoken from the pulpit of *Moriah Chapel* changed Evan's life. The phrase, *"What would Jesus do?"* became his obsession.

- He repeatedly asked himself, *"What have I done for Jesus?"* as he further dedicated himself to the work of the Lord.

Evan was so intense on giving his life to God that he read everything he could, pertaining to Him. He used his earnings to purchase instruments that he later learned to play. In fact, he was able to succeed at most everything he put his hand to because he put his whole heart into it.

He excelled in any business apprenticeship offered to him, and he excelled in personal character. He was also a prolific writer, having several of his poems and essays published in local newspapers. #2

December of 1903

Evan knew in his heart that God had planned a great revival for the Welsh community. While preaching at Moriah he said, *"I have reached out my hand and touched the flame. I am burning and waiting for a sign."*

It is understood that Evan Roberts and other young ministry students were required to listen to great men of their denomination and pattern their preaching styles after them. But Evan was an exception. Though he had been accepted into the bible college, he couldn't complete his studies because of his burning desire to preach and pray. #3

According to historian Dr. J Edwin Orr, Seth Joshua, a Presbyterian evangelist, visited Newcastle Emlyn College in Wales where Evan Roberts was preparing for the ministry. *(Roberts was 26 years old when he felt the call to preach.)*

During Seth Joshua's visit to the college, the students **were stirred to a deep desire for prayer** *(it's said that for thirteen years Evan was always in prayer, and in prayer meetings)* and asked if they could attend.

It was there, the students heard Seth Joshua pray passionately, ***"O God, bend us."*** Immediately the Spirit of God bore witness to young Evan, *"This is what you need."* Evan was gripped with the spirit of intercession. ***"I fell on*** *my knees with my arms over the seat in front of me and the tears flowed freely. I cried, 'Bend me! Bend me! Bend us!'"* Perspiration poured down my face and tears streamed quickly – until I thought that the blood came out.

"I am coming, coming Lord to Thee!"

Now a great burden came upon him for the salvation of lost souls, a great sense of God's love, and his own unworthiness. He said, he had a vision of all Wales being lifted up to Heaven, and began to desire a little band and go all over the country *(Wales)* preaching.

"Bend the Church and save the world..."
Cried the young Welsh Miner, with
All the passion of his prayer burdened
Heart; and God did.

When the meeting with Seth Joshua concluded, Roberts returned to the college with his classmates but found he couldn't concentrate on his studies. Something was happening in his heart. *"I keep hearing a voice?"* Roberts told his principal, *"that tells me I must go home to speak to the young people in my church."* Roberts wondered if it was the voice of the devil or the **voice of the Spirit.** The principal answered, *"the devil never gives orders like that. You can have a week off."*

It's important to remember that for many years revival had been the passion of his heart. He said, *"I could sit up all night to read or talk about revivals. It was the Spirit that moved me to think about revival."*

Overwhelmed in the Presence

At times he was overwhelmed by the presence of God. On occasions his body trembled until his bed was shaken. One night his brother Dan awoke and shouted, *"Are you ill, Evan?"* The truth was that for weeks he enjoyed times of rare and intimate communion with God in the night watches, such as few are privileged to enjoy. All this was behind that prayer from his heart of *"Bend me!"*

On the 31st October, Evan Roberts felt a strong leading from the Lord to return to Loughor. He told his mother and brother, *"There will be a great change in Loughor in less than a fortnight, we are going to have the greatest revival that Wales has ever seen."*

Young Roberts returned to Loughor and told his pastor he had come home to preach. The pastor was far from comfortable, however, allowing this inexperienced student to address the entire congregation, so he suggested Evan Roberts testify at the prayer meeting on Monday night. Evan agreed, thankful that at least he would have opportunity to speak to some of the congregation.

On the first of November, attendance was greater than expected at the meeting. The pastor decided not to call on Evan Roberts until the very end. Just before people were ready to depart, the pastor said, *"Our young brother, Evan Roberts, feels he has a message for you, if you care to wait."*

Only seventeen people remained. He *(Evan)* spoke on the importance of being filled with the Holy Spirit. Saying,

*"Revival comes from a knowledge of the Holy Spirit
and the way of co-working with Him which enables
Him to work in revival power."*

Roberts told those present: *"I have a message for you from
God."* This consisted of four great points, which became such
an important part of his message! Giving the challenge, *"Do
you desire an outpouring of the Spirit?"*

Keys to Revival

The message;

- "Is there sin in your past that you have not confessed
  to God? On your knees at once. Your past must be put
  away and yourself cleansed."

- "Is there anything in your life that is doubtful? Have
  you forgiven everybody, everybody, EVERYBODY? If
  not, don't expect forgiveness for your own sins, you
  won't get it."

- "Do what the Spirit prompts you to do. Obedience
  – prompt, implicit, unquestioning obedience to the
  Spirit."

- "A public confession of Christ as your Saviour. There is
  a vast difference between profession and confession."

According to eyewitnesses, by 10 P.M. all seventeen had
responded. The pastor was so moved he asked Evan Roberts
if he would be willing to speak at the Missions service the
following night. Then he asked him to share at the regular

Wednesday night meeting. A fourth service was scheduled the following night, and still another. It was decided to continue a second week when the heavens seemed to open.

Soon the main road on which the church was located was packed solid with hungry seekers coming to the service. Shopkeepers even closed early so they too could get a seat in the large but packed church.

Evan taught the people to pray, *"Send the Spirit now for Christ's sake."* People were astonished at his holy boldness!

Prayer was the Order of the Day

The whole neighbourhood was stirred. People did not go to work but attended the early Morning Prayer meeting, which lasted four hours. Immense crowds poured into the town and in the evening service, Evan Roberts announced a hymn, which became one of the revival hymns: *"Heavenly Jesus, ride victorious, gird thy sword upon thy thigh."* Praise and prayer broke out spontaneously, Roberts walking through the chapel clapping his hands in holy ecstasy.

At a most intense moment in the service he proclaimed that a mighty revival was coming to ALL Wales and that they in Aberdare were only opening the gates for it. From Aberdare, Evan Roberts moved around the towns up and down the valleys of South Wales.

- The presence of God was felt everywhere.
- The atmosphere was divinely charged.

A miner who was converted in the revival once described it in the following graphic way.

He said, *"that he had been in the revival and he had also on one occasion been in an underground explosion in one of the local pits and there was not much to choose between the two!"*

The atmosphere underground was charged with dust and methane gas, and the atmosphere in Wales in the revival was impregnated with the presence of God.

It's said that Evan's services were marked with laughing, crying, dancing, joy and brokenness. Soon, the newspapers began covering them, and the revival became a national story. Some of the reporters themselves were converted at the meetings. The revival spread with great fervour throughout Wales.

- Soon bars and movie houses closed.
- Former prostitutes started holding bible studies.
- People began to pay their longstanding debts.
- And those who once selfishly wasted their money on alcohol suddenly became a great joy and support to their families.

The Wales revival meetings had no choirs or **special ceremonies.** There were **no offerings, no hymnbooks, no committees, no song leaders,** and **no paid advertising.** Leaders from denominations who were hungry for God attended the meetings. **It is said that in one city, all the**

ministers exchanged pulpits for a day in an effort to break down denominational walls and establish unity. Even the women of Wales had been banned from any public role in church life, but now could be seen praying and praising openly. Eventually Evan even encouraged national and racial barriers to be broken. #4

Civic leaders met to discuss what to do with the police now that crime had disappeared. In one community, the sergeant of the police was asked by a reporter, *"What do you do with your time?"* *"Before the revival,"* he replied, *"We had two main jobs, to prevent crime and to control crowds attending soccer games. Since the revival there is practically no crime. So we just go with crowds."*

When asked what he meant, the sergeant replied, *"You know where the crowds are. They are filling the churches!"* "But how does that affect the police?" asked the reporter, *"We have seventeen police in our station,"* replied the sergeant. *"Five do nothing but control crowds on their way to prayer meetings."*

"What about the other twelve?" "Oh, we've organised three quartets with those officers," the sergeant responded. "They sing at the churches. If any church wants a quartet, they just call the police station."

Critics were Many

However, the Welsh revival had many critics because of the emotional scenes and manifestations. Evan Roberts was at the centre of the revival. In 1905 he wrote in response to fierce criticism by those opposed to displays of emotion in church:

He writes;

"The Power of the revival in South Wales is not of men, but of God. God has *'made me glad,'* and I am showing others the great joy of serving Him, a joy so great and so wonderful that I shall never be able to express it in its completeness.

I have been asked concerning my methods. I have none. I never prepare the words I shall speak. I leave all that to Him. I am not the source of this revival. I am only one agent in what is growing to be a multitude. I am not moving men's hearts and changing men's lives; not I, but *'God worketh in me.'*

His Spirit came to me one night, when upon my knees I asked Him for guidance, and five months later I was baptised with the Spirit. I know that the work, which has been done through me, is not due to any human ability that I possess. It is His work and to His glory." #5

Media-spread Fire

The controversy at that time and the massive media coverage helped fan the flames of the Holy Spirit. News of what was happening **soon spread to other nations.** The people of **South Africa, Russia, India, Ireland, Norway, Canada,** and **Holland** rushed to Wales. Many came to carry a portion of this revival back to their own nations.

It is said that during this time, the Californian evangelist and journalist, Frank Bartleman, **wrote to Evan and asked how to bring revival to America.** Evan corresponded several times with Bartleman, each time listing principles for revival while encouraging him to pursue it, and assuring him of the prayers from Wales. Bartleman would later become instrumental in recording the events of the Azusa Street Revival that originated in Southern California in 1906. There is no doubt that the revival in Wales started a worldwide hunger for God. #6

Evan Roberts Continues

"Some things have been said about our meetings, and about me which are not true (Evan reported); but God's truth has not been hurt by these misstatements, and they, therefore, matter little. I believe too, that He has put it into the hearts of those who have written of the revival to say helpful things, for some of the papers have carried our message to many whom we have not personally reached.

I believe that the world is upon the threshold of a great religious revival, and I pray daily that I may be allowed to help bring this about. Wonderful things have happened in Wales in a few weeks, but these are only a beginning. **The world will be swept by His Spirit as by a rushing mighty wind."**

By this time when all this fierce criticism was raging, the revival was really under way and throughout that year *(1905)* there was no stopping it. For two glorious years the Welsh churches were crowded out.

A hundred thousand outsiders were converted and added to the churches, the vast majority remaining true to the end, says Edwin Orr in the Re-Study of Revival and Revivalism.

The whole of Wales was now affected. Hardened unbelievers were gloriously converted. Drunkards, thieves, gamblers were transformed. Confessions of awful sins were heard on every side. Old debts were paid. Miners prayed together before commencing their shifts in the coalmines. Pit ponies unused to the new kindness and clean language, without the usual kicks and curses, almost stopped work until they got adjusted. Courts had few cases to try, whole football and rugby teams got converted and fixtures were abandoned.

The young men were more concerned with praying than playing! Dance halls were deserted, the pubs were empty and a few went out of business, but the prayer meetings were crowded.

David Matthews in his eyewitness account describes the services, "Such marvellous singing, quite extempore *(without preparation; off-hand)*, could only be created by a supernatural power – the Holy Spirit. No choir, no conductor, no organ – just spontaneous, unctionised soul-singing.

Once the first hymn was given out, the meeting conducted itself. There was no leader, but people felt an unseen control. Singing, sobbing, praying intermingled and proceeded without intermission."

❖

CHAPTER 2

Church Leaders Attack

As in every revival there are some extravagances, some fanaticism, but the main work is glorious with lasting results. However, Evan Roberts found himself once more under severe attack, this time from other church leaders.

The main attack on his motives and methods came by a congregational minister, Peter Price. This appeared in the correspondence columns of the Western Mail on January 31st, and initiated a protracted and heated public debate, although Roberts himself took no part in it. Price claimed that there were two revivals, one true and the other false.

The former had been in progress for as long as two years, his own church at Dowlais having been blessed with an increase of some hundreds in the previous five or six months. The Evan Roberts Movement, on the other hand, was *"a sham, a mockery, a blasphemous travesty of the real thing."* The former, *"the gloriously real revival,"* was of the devil. #7

So-called *"Excesses"*

Another scathing attack on the so-called *"excesses"* of the Welsh revival was published just four years later in 1909.

Here are some extracts:

The neighbourhood of Part Talbot was once noted as the place that could supply characters capable of working up these wondrous religious spectacles. These itinerant devotees were in the habit of attending various religious gathering with the expectation of being *"touched."* The congregation knew beforehand what to expect and the special preacher for the occasion did not at all resent their appearance, and even shot his arrows with a view to the desired end.

There could be heard a deep wail, then a piercing cry; the next moment a woman would be casting off her bonnet, raising her arm, and throwing everything into disorder and confusion. Others would catch the infection; and there would be no attempt at checking such manifestations, for the common people took pleasure in them, and the preacher looked on with a complacent smile. Some of those who were affected during the Revival kept it on for months afterwards, giving way to violent emotions when the preacher reached a certain point.

Such characters have been known to interrupt preachers during the delivery of a sermon and to completely overcome them, to the annoyance of the congregation and detriment of the service. Such scenes have occurred repeatedly since the last Welsh Revival. But there have been strong personalities in the pulpit, who have successfully resisted such interruptions, thus proving beyond a doubt that such paroxysms *(fits)* are largely a matter of encouragement.

On what principle are we to explain such violent bodily exercises? Have they any spiritual significance? Had they any divine message? My belief is that they were purely physical. They did not possess any specific spiritual value, and did not convey any moral lesson!

True, there is much in the action of the Divine Spirit that eludes our grasp and which no philosophy can ever hope to fully explain. But those wild cries of horror, which were so fearful in their violence during the Revival, were undoubtedly due to mental action, to sympathy, to the power of suggestion and physical causes.

The press worked the sentimentality of the Revival for all that it was worth. It was a harvest-time for publishers and journalists. There was money in it, and unfortunately there has always been money in Welsh sentiment. There is more wealth to be coined out of the feelings of this people than out of their judgement. Now that the Revival passion is gone, and with the passion the profits that were in it, publishers take no further interest in the Movement. #8

As James A. Stewart says, *"Bend the Church and save the world,"* is the secret of every true awakening.

Here is part of a prayer that Evan Roberts prayed in one of the great revival meetings in one of the towns where over thirteen hundred new converts were rejoicing in their new found faith;

> *Lord Jesus, help us now through the Holy Spirit to come face to face with the cross. Whatever the hindrances may be, we commit the service to Thee. Put us all under the blood. Oh, Lord, place the blood on all our past up to this moment. We thank Thee for the blood. In the name of Jesus Christ, bind the devil this moment. We point to the cross of Christ, Oh, open the heavens. Descend upon us now. We shall give all the glory to Thy Name. No one else has a right to the glory but Thee – take it, Lord. Glorify Thy Son in this meeting. Oh, Holy Spirit, do Thy work through us and in us now. Speak Thy word in power for Thy Name's sake.*
>
> *Amen and Amen!* #9

Confusion and Collapse

In 1905, Evan Robert's mind became confused. He often said that he wanted to enter into the *"sufferings of the Master."* Sometimes, he would start a service in gentleness and joy, then suddenly jump up, wave his arms, and sharply rebuke those who weren't pure in heart. Then he would threaten to leave the service.

He commented to his friend, Sidney Evans that he was afraid of speaking words that weren't of God. He heard many voices, and sometimes he wasn't sure which was God's and which was his. He was also constantly examining himself for any un-confessed sin. His number one fear was that people would exalt him instead of God.

As the revival continued and specific needs became apparent, Evan began to operate in the gifts of the Spirit. Out of ignorance, the people labelled Evan **telepathic,** since they didn't understand how he could be so spiritually accurate. **But instead of stopping to teach the people concerning the gifts of the Spirit, Evan simply continued to operate in them.**

At times, Evan would name a specific sin that was present and call for immediate repentance. Other times, he would know of a person outside the building agonising before God. Evan would abruptly leave the building, head out into the street, and find that person on his knees crying to God.

The voices Evan was hearing began to trouble him greatly. **But instead of receiving counsel from mature leaders,** he chose to continue following the signs and to ignore the uneasiness within.

It was at this time that *Evan Roberts suffered his first emotional collapse.* He was forced to remain in the home of a friend and cancel his meetings.

Obstacles Arriving and Departing

When the people heard of his cancellation, they were outraged and offended. Though still severely fatigued, Evan was **swayed by their pressure** and rescheduled the meetings. But as to be expected, at the meeting he was hazy in mind and rebuked the crowd sharply. He even began to point out *"obstacles arriving"* and *"obstacles departing."* The people became concerned with the conflict he was pointing out rather than with their hunger for God.

After this, complaints and criticism abounded against Evan from every corner of Wales. They labelled him a *"hypnotist," "exhibitionist,"* and *"occultist."* In retaliation, Evan began to condemn entire congregations for the cold hearts of one or two who would show up at his meetings. He once even condemned a man's *"soul"* forbidding anyone to pray for him.

Accusation and criticism spread like wildfire. Every day produced new, bitter charges in the newspapers and letters. And each new meeting was filled with challenging agnostics who called him a *"bearer of false fire"* or *"profaner."* Friends tried to justify his actions, saying he was a young, inexperienced minister and subject to making *"a young man's mistake."*

Soon Evan Roberts suffered another physical and emotional breakdown. Much to his critics' delight, Evan cancelled all his meetings. He was branded as unbalanced, and revival converts began to wonder if Satan had deceived them. In response to the outburst, a psychologist who examined Evan published this remark: *"Our organisms can't support such pitiless tensions and violent repeated shocks, shaking the nerves and exhausting the brain and body."* With this, Evan went into silence for a season. #10

The critical point of Evan Roberts' downfall came when he returned to northern Wales in the summer of 1906. He was asked to participate in a **Keswick-type Easter Convention** for ministers and church leaders. **It was there that Evan spoke on what he called his new burden,** which was the **identification with Christ through suffering.** Soon afterwards, he became tremendously overstrained and broke down again.

Enter Jezebel

At the Keswick meeting, Mrs. Jessie Penn-Lewis introduced herself to Evan. Mrs. Penn-Lewis was a socially influential and wealthy woman from England. She was also a minister, but the Welsh due to serious doctrinal conflicts had scorned her ministry. **They rejected her *"suffering"* teachings and abolished her ministry in their nation.**

When Mrs. Penn-Lewis heard Evan's message on the cross, she aligned herself with him **to gain his acceptance.** And she confided to friends that *she felt Evan had too, been shattered and would need some type of getaway.* **Then she convinced Evan of her position, while pointing out his excellent teaching,** and that **the abuses he was suffering is because of it. In his weakened condition, Evan succumbed to her influence. Less than a month after being constantly paired with Penn-Lewis, Evan suffered his fourth and most serious nervous breakdown.**

Newly discovered letters show that Penn-Lewis had ulterior motives with Evan Roberts. **She used his name repeatedly while exonerating her own methods and beliefs.** She also told the ministers of Wales that she was so hurt by their opinion of her and her doctrine that she wouldn't return to their nation. And she added that it was best for Evan to stay away from Wales because he, like her, was too shattered to do anything.

After this announcement by Penn-Lewis, she transported Roberts quickly and quietly from his beloved homeland and place of his call. **Penn-Lewis and her husband retired Evan to their estate in England called Woodlands. Then they built their new home around Evan Roberts' needs. They built him a *bedroom*, a *prayer room*, and his own private *stairway*.** It was here that the great evangelist was confined to bed.

Denouncing the Gifts

While at Woodlands, Penn-Lewis visited Evan daily. Evan listened respectfully as she told him of the mistakes and wrong judgements she felt he made while in the ministry. But Evan wasn't able to discern that everything the woman said was based entirely on her opinions.

As Penn-Lewis sat by Evan's bedside she questioned him about the supernatural gift that operated through him. She determined that Evan's depression was caused from this spiritual operation. **Denouncing these gifts given to Evan,** Penn-Lewis lectured that unless he was totally crucified to self, he was deceived.

Filled with condemnation, **Evan finally agreed that all the supernatural operations he had experienced couldn't have been of God.** Besides confounding the multitudes, Evan concluded that he too, had been deceived by the supernatural operations.

From this point on, Evan determined from Mrs. Penn-Lewis' counsel that he would no longer trust any moving of the supernatural. And he concluded that in order for the

Holy Spirit to move through any believer, he or she would have to have a far greater wisdom and experience than that which he possessed. The depressed revivalist's condition was extremely frail and was further frustrated by the repeated prodding and drilling of Penn-Lewis.

I wonder if Evan ever considered the thousands that turned to God and became born again because of these gifts. Could he remember the multitudes that came from other nations to receive from his ministry and carry it to their countries? No doubt he heard of their glowing reports in their own nations.

I wonder if the thought of the multitudes, hungry for a touch, who stood in the streets because he had been so transparent for the Holy Spirit to use. Did he ever once consider that his lack of rest – not lack of concentration – caused his confusion? Did he think the mistakes he made from exhaustion summed the total fruit of his ministry?

If Evan Roberts ever did consider these things, the thought never turned to action. Thus, the spiritual equipment that came as a result of his call was severely damaged for any future manifestations. #11

Spiritual Manipulation

The Church has so many Penn-Lewis types, who seemingly don't care who they manipulate. Spiritual manipulation is common in any new God ordained work; the goal of course is to stop the move of God. Remember though where there is a Jezebel you usually find an **Ahab!**

You could say the **Jezebel spirit** primarily works through women or effeminate men. The **Lucifer spirit** will attach itself in most cases to men.

Before the fall of mankind through Adam and Eve, Lucifer was in the inner circle of leadership. He was very religious, gifted, powerful, influential and strong-willed.

- Lucifer means "light-bearer" or "star."

- Jezebel in the Hebrew means, "Where is Baal?"

- Both usurped authority *(Isaiah 14)*.

- Both were unhappy in subordinate roles *(they want to be number one)*.

- Both were wily, scheming, opposing and deceptive.

- These spirits are attracted to strong prophetic, charismatic, Faith churches but are found to some degree in all Christian churches.

They will work through some of the nicest people you've ever met. Gifted, loyal, giving, praying, volunteering people who look like an answer to prayer, and they may be at first. But because of a character flaw, a wound that never healed or some other dysfunctional trait that was underground for a season, they then become easy prey for these spirits. You won't pick up a potential problem unless your discerner is working.

Usually people with these spirits start the climb into leadership. They try to get real chummy with the pastor and his wife. They do and say all the right things. Again we must remember to read Ephesians 6:16,

> *Above all, taking the shield of faith with which you will be able to quench all the fiery darts of the wicked one.*

Characteristic Signs

In most cases the persons involved with these spirits are victims who are being used by the devil to victimise. Deception is a very strong force, not to be underestimated.

Here are some warning-sign-characteristics of people being used by the Lucifer and Jezebel spirits:

- Look for authority without much responsibility.
- Always warn you about other leaders.
- Give special gifts to the pastor/spouse.
- Ask you to bend the rules for them every now and then.
- Start to have their own *"following."*
- Don't show up on Sunday if some big shot is preaching at another church.
- Give irregularly.
- Always have a *"word"* for you *(a letter).*
- Need constant attention.
- Want desperately to be an elder *(or leadership position).*
- They are always on your mind!

The most common places for these spirits to work are in home bible studies, prayer groups, cliques or any other gathering place off church grounds. This does not mean we shouldn't have home cell or care groups in our churches, but it does tell us to know what's going on and who is in leadership.

New converts can't and won't hurt you. They're just glad to be saved and accepted. It's the dissatisfied. **The one who needs appreciation and attention.** The church hopper who has *"seen it all," "heard it all"* and was *"sent by God"* to help you.

Be extremely cautious of people who tell you all that is wrong with their former church and pastor, and how they tried to help but no one would listen, so God led them out. Also be careful of the person God is always *"talking to."* *"Super spiritual"* people are usually super-flaky and can be a super problem!

All Ministries have Problems

We all miss it now and again. Some of the greatest preachers in the world have blundered, but what makes them great is how, with integrity, they handle their mistakes. God gives grace to the humble, but resists the proud. God in His Word does not just let us see the patriarchs and matriarchs of faith succeed, but He gives us a peek into their failures. This is to give us all hope that grace and mercy do indeed follow the upright.

Dr. C M Ward, once told me *(he said this to Dick Bernal)*, *"Son, confess your sins to God and your faults to man." He went on to add; "Only God can truly forgive and forget. Man struggles in that area and as David said, 'Lord, against you and you only have I sinned.'"*

David's dilemma in Psalm 41 is that his enemies, even former friends, were trying to use his mistakes to destroy him. God judges to deliver, but the spirits of Lucifer and Jezebel judge to condemn and destroy.

You can tell the truth about someone and still bring a curse on yourself if your motive is to hurt or discredit that individual. Truth is a two-edged sword. Like a surgeon's knife, it can cut to heal or like an enemy's sword, it can cut to kill.

Bear your soul to very few outside of your Spouse

There are those around you who will use it against you. I'm not being paranoid; I'm just sharing out of personal experience says, Pastor Dick Bernal, and that of hundreds of pastors I know. I've seen it happen over and over again.

Our greatest strength is to be transparent, open and honest, this can be taken by some as a weakness or carnality. **Choose your staff and friends with care and prayer.** #12

Dr. Roberts Liardon adds, "The life of Evan Roberts was complex. I find it interesting that even though Penn-Lewis used Evan's ministry influence for her own ulterior motives, Evan obviously allowed it. In the beginning, he probably had little choice because of his invalid-like condition. **However, the young revivalist remained in her household for eight years.** And this leaves me with a multitude of questions.

- Was the Penn-Lewis home a comfort zone for him?
- Did he lose all confidence in his public image?
- Why didn't he go home?
- Did his emotional breakdowns cause him to feel secure with someone else in control?

The only thing we can conclude for sure is that Evan Roberts made a choice to leave the public fore front. And the Penn-Lewis home is where he wanted to be." #13

The most formative result of the Welsh revival was the creation of a widespread spirit of expectation for still greater things. Men justly asked: Why Wales only? Why not other lands? Why not a World Wide Revival?

Prayer to that end received a tremendous new impetus. And while so many were interceding for a wider outpouring of the Holy Spirit, others were pleading equally for a deeper work. Faith was rising to visualise a return to "Apostolic Christianity" in all its pristine beauty and power. #14

❖

CHAPTER 3

Different Days Different Ways

Researching carefully the after math of the 1904 Revival, most notable of such researchers being Edwin Orr. **He has proved conclusively that the Welsh Revival, far from being confined to Wales, "was the furthest reaching of all the Movements of the awakening.** For it affected the whole evangelical course in India, Korea and China, renewed revivals in Japan and South Africa, and sent a wave of awakening over Africa, Latin America and the South Seas" *(Edwin Orr).*

The rest of Britain was also affected, the Awakening of 1905 *"affected each of the counties of England;"* the happenings may not have been quite as explosive as those in Wales but they were extraordinary nevertheless.

The spicing of the Pentecostal Movement in the Welsh Revival of 1904; such great *Pentecostal evangelists as*

Stephen and George Jeffreys were raised up in the years, which followed. Not to mention such time-honoured servants of God as John Thomas and John Daniel Jones and a host of others with world-affecting ministries, who were very much the *"children of the revival."*

Stephen and George Jeffreys

Stephen and George Jeffreys were born in a small village in Wales *(1876-1943 --- 1889-1962)*. Since Wales at that time was world famous for coal, their father and all of their relatives were coal miners. However, the Jeffreys were religious people, open to know more about God and to grow spiritually.

What started Stephen down the path of becoming one of the most unusual ministers of the entire twentieth century was a vision that appeared in their church in Wales. **This vision involved a bleeding lamb.** About three hundred people came to see this phenomenon.

Stephen was so fascinated by it that he lay down on the floor under the vision and cried out to God for three days about the needs of the world, especially physical healing for people.

He felt the anointing of the Lord come upon him. And when he left the church building, he found that when he prayed for people, they were miraculously healed. Within a short time, any building he rented was immediately filled to overflowing. In some cities, people would stand in line as long as three days to get into the building.

46

Stephen Jeffreys was a man of iron. He would sing and preach and pray for the sick, then go to a nearby hotel and eat and sleep for two or three hours. During that time his workers cleared the auditorium, got everyone out, and opened the front doors. No one paid attention to whether it was 11 at night or 2 in the morning. After two or three hours of rest, Stephen would come back and repeat his singing, preaching, and praying.

In the middle of a service, Stephen would jump off the platform, run to the back, curse rheumatoid arthritis, for example, and scream, *"Come out of him."* People said you could hear bones pop for approximately thirty feet around as the person's bones began to relocate.

One night when a young man came along with one leg that just dangled, because it had never grown, Stephen Jeffreys put him on the platform and said, *"Leg! I tell you, grow, in Jesus' name!"* Thousands of people watched as that young man's leg grew out eighteen inches, the people went berserk. They jumped. They ran. They screamed!

Difficult to stay Humble

When people are healed through prayer, it is sometimes very difficult to stay humble, because people praise you, adore you, and give you all the money they have. Stephen became very wealthy.

- **It is said that Stephen Jeffreys stood before thousands of people in Africa saying, *"Ladies and gentlemen, the world is at my feet to worship me."***

He continued **to preach his very simple sermons** for some time, and they still were followed by remarkable healings. **But the wealth began to affect him. In order to look more like a minister and less like a coal miner, he began to wear the attire of a Roman Catholic priest with vestments.**

In 1936, however, Stephen was sick. He had rheumatoid arthritis. His head and neck were kinked over. His arms were twisted and his shoulders were twisted.

Lester Sumrall on the Scene

Lester Sumrall went to visit him in Wales. As tears ran down his face, he said, *"I'm sorry to have let this number one thing that I delivered people from come upon me."*

- Mr. Sumrall said, *"I'm so glad to meet you. I have heard of all of your great revivals, and I have met people healed in those revivals in America, Australia, and different places. I just had to come see you."*

- He said, *"Lester, it has been weeks since any preacher has come into this room. Not one pastor whom I gave a church to has come to see me."*

- *"That is all right, God sends in those who have a craving for the same kind of anointing that you used to have. I want you to know I will remember this day as one of the happiest in my life."*

For several hours, Mr. Sumrall stayed and enjoyed the presence of a man who once operated under a great anointing and power, **although he had lost it. Later, Sumrall asked his mentor, Howard Cater, how this could happen.**

- He said, *"Lester, God will not permit His servants to have the gold or the glory"* [that belongs to Him].

Out of possible ignorance, this boy from the mines of Wales **accepted the glory that was lavished upon him by thousands of people.** He died soon after that. Stephen had started numerous churches out of revivals, but not one of the pastors from those churches ever came to see him in his last illness.

- Mr. Sumrall says, *"I learned from his example possibly one of the greatest lessons of my ministry. I try to pass it on to those young men who look to me for advice: **Stephen Jeffreys lost his power because no one had taught him not to touch God's gold or His glory."***

A Different Brother, a Different Pitfall

George Jeffreys travelled with Stephen as his music director. Then he discovered that he was anointed with the same remarkable strength and power as his brother. However, there was a difference in their personalities. Stephen was exuberant, joyful, and a singing person, while George was sober, dark and handsome.

George raised up *Foursquare Churches*, while Stephen raised up dozens of *Assemblies of God Churches*. There was no animosity or fighting – it just became two different highways for their lives.

George Jeffreys had a deep voice. He held meetings in the Royal Albert Hall in London, seating ten thousand or more people. It was jam packed, and hundreds could not be seated. It is likely that George became more popular than his brother did, for the simple reason he was so much more capable of organising and handling funds. **He handled funds that came in through an organisation, while Stephen ran the money into his own bank account.**

George Jeffreys' eyes were like fire. When he was at the Royal Albert Hall he could see that mighty congregation of more than ten thousand at one time. He knew their needs, and when he prayed, miracles happened – not as great as when his brother, Stephen, prayed possibly, but wonderful healings took place.

When someone in the royal family became sick, it was George Jeffreys whom they called, and they would pick him up in a limousine to come pray for the person who was sick. He was a very diplomatic man, however, **and not a** *"name dropper"* **at all.**

Lost Tribes of Israel

George Jeffreys also got off track when he read a book that caused him to believe that England was one of the lost tribes of Israel. When he taught this, at least half his pastors and churches left him. **After a worldwide ministry, this erroneous teaching resulted in George going into seclusion.**

The glory departed from George's life because he went after a cult and left the divine truth he had been taught from childhood. He went with the interpretation of men rather than staying with the teachings of the bible.

Pioneers of Faith

In his book **Pioneers of Faith** on page 95, Lester Sumrall says **"I tell preachers all the time that there are three things they must watch: pride, material things and sex. God hates pride. There are outstanding men in the religious world in our country, but you cannot get to them for the simple reason they feel they are so important.**

When you are successful, material gain will come to you. God wants you to be a channel. He does not want to build a dam and make you into a lake where nothing can go out but everything comes in. **The Dead Sea is dead because it has no outlet.**

Every minister of God must not only be a receiver, but he must be a giver. **With greed or lust you can lose your relationship with God.**

Most preachers are so innocent, they do not know that if they have a church with five hundred people, there may be a minimum of ten women who would give their souls to sleep with them just one night. They idolise their pastors. For them, to have sex with the pastor would be the greatest achievement of their whole lives.

A minister of the gospel must remember that he is a servant of a mighty God, and he is a servant of the people. **He is not great.** *Only God is great.* I have never met a minister who fell into adultery who intended to sin, or who set out to do this.

Joseph in the Old Testament was a **type** of the Lord Jesus Christ because he kept himself straight in all three of these areas.

When George Jeffreys died, there were only two lines in the newspaper: *'George Jeffreys, an English evangelist, died on such–and–such a date'* – a sad ending to great beginnings for a pair of brothers." #15

Formulation and Doctrine

At around the same time as the Welsh revival, a similar revival broke out in Los Angeles. In many ways there are similarities here with what happened in Toronto, London, Lakeland and elsewhere. The revival was charismatic in theology; the leaders at first had little idea how to manage the phenomena responsibly.

The media played a central role in advertising the meetings through their own reporting, people travelled thousands of miles to go there, and the manifestations mainly attracted believers.

Thus, back to the time of the Pentecostal outbreak in America in 1901, there had been at least a century of Movements emphasising a second blessing called the baptism in the Holy Spirit. In America, such Keswick teachers as A.B Simpson and A.J Gordon also added an emphasis on divine healing.

The first Pentecostal churches in the world originated in the Holiness Movement before 1901. It would not be an overstatement to say that 20th century Pentecostalism, at least in America, was born in a Holiness cradle.

We have already established that the First Pentecostals, in the modern sense of the word, can be traced to Parham's bible school in Topeka, Kansas, in 1901. In spite of controversy over the origins and timing of Parham's emphasis on tongues, all historians agree the Movement began early in 1901 just as the world entered the 20th century. As a result of this Topeka Pentecost, Parham formulated the doctrine that Tongues was the *"bible evidence"* of the baptism in the Holy Spirit.

Teaching that tongues was a supernatural impartation of human languages for the purpose of world evangelization, Parham also advocated that missionaries need not study foreign languages, since they would be able to preach in miraculous tongues all over the world.

Armed with this new theology, Parham founded a Church Movement called the *"Apostolic Faith"* and began a whirlwind revival tour of the Midwest to promote his new experience *(which we read about in "The Early Years - Anointed Generals, Past and Present" Part One)*.

Azusa, world wide Attention

It was not until 1906, however, that Pentecostalism achieved worldwide attention. This came through the ***Azusa Street Revival in Los Angeles***, led by Pastor William Joseph Seymour. Seymour first learned about the baptism in the Holy Spirit with tongues in 1905 at a bible school Parham held in Houston.

In 1906, Seymour was invited to pastor a black Holiness church in Los Angeles. The historic Azusa meetings began in

April 1906 in a former African Methodist Episcopal Church building at 312 Azusa Street in downtown Los Angeles.

Frank Bartleman was at the heart of what happened in Los Angeles. This is what he wrote shortly after the 1905 revival began:

When we began to pray in the spring of 1905, no one seemed to have much faith for anything out of the ordinary. April 15, the Lord called me to ten days of special prayer. I felt greatly burdened but had no idea of what He had particularly in mind. Wednesday, April 18, the terrible San Francisco earthquake came, which also devastated the surrounding country. No less than ten thousand lost their lives in Francisco alone.

I felt a deep conviction that the Lord was hearing our prayers for a revival in His own way. A tremendous burden of prayer came on me that the people might not be indifferent to His voice.

Thursday, April 19, while sitting in the noon meeting at Peniel, 227 South Main Street the floor suddenly began to move beneath us. Many people ran into the middle of the street, looking up anxiously at the buildings, fearing they were about to fall.

I went home and after a season of prayer was pressed of the Lord to go to the meeting which had been moved from Bonnie Brae Street to 312 Azusa Street. Here they had rented an old frame building, formerly a Methodist church, in the centre of the city, now a long time out of use for meetings. It was my first visit to *"Azusa Mission."*

I gave a message at my first meeting at *"Azusa."* Two of the saints spoke in *"tongues."* Much blessing seemed to attend the utterance. It was soon noised abroad that God was working at Azusa. All classes began to flock to the meetings. Many were curious and unbelieving, but others were hungry for God.

Persecution never hurts God's Work

The newspapers began to ridicule and abuse the meetings, thus giving much free advertising. This brought the crowds. The devil overdid himself again. Outside persecution never hurt the work. I had the most to fear from the working of evil spirits within.

Keen spiritualists and hypnotists came to investigate, and to try their influence. Then all the religious sore heads and crooks and cranks came, seeking a place in the work. We had the most to fear from these. But this is always the danger to every new work. They have no place elsewhere.

This condition cast a fear over many, which was hard to overcome. It hindered the Spirit much. Many were afraid to seek God, for fear the devil might get them. We found early in the *"Azusa"* work that when we attempted to steady the Ark the Lord stopped working. We dared not call the attention of the people too much to the working of the devil. Fear would follow. We could only pray. Then God gave victory. There was a presence of God with us through prayer we could depend on.

The leaders had a limited experience, and the wonder is the work survived at all against its powerful adversaries. But it was of God. That was the secret. I found the earthquake had opened many hearts.

The work was getting clearer and stronger at *"Azusa."* God was working mightily. It seemed that everyone had to go to Azusa. Missionaries were gathered there from Africa, India, and the islands of the sea. Preachers and workers had crossed the continent, and come from distant islands, with an irresistible drawing to Los Angeles. *"Gather my saints together."* They had come up for *"Pentecost,"* though they little realised it. It was God's call.

Holiness meetings, tents and missions began to close up for lack of attendance. Their people were at *"Azusa."* Brother and Sister Garr closed the *"Burning Bush"* hall, came to *"Azusa,"* received the *"baptism,"* and were soon on their way to India to spread the fire. Even Brother Smale had to come to *"Azusa,"* to look up his members. He invited them back home, promised them liberty in the Spirit, and for a time God wrought mightily at the New Testament Church also.

Much Persecution, especially from the Press

They wrote us up shamefully, but this only drew the crowds. Some gave the work six months to live. Soon the meetings were running day and night. The place was packed out nightly. The whole building, upstairs and down had now been cleared and put into use. There were far more white people than coloured coming.

Someone might be speaking. Suddenly the Spirit would fall upon the congregation. God Himself would give the altar call; men would fall all over the house, like the slain in battle, or rush for the altar, all at once, to seek God. The scene often resembled a forest of fallen trees. Such a scene cannot be imitated. I never saw an altar call given in those early days. God Himself would call them. And the preacher knew when to quit.

When He spoke we all obeyed. It seemed a fearful thing to hinder or grieve the Spirit. The whole place was steeped in prayer. God was in His Holy Temple. It was for man to keep silent. *The Shekinah Glory rested there.* In fact some claim to have seen the glory by night over the building. I do not doubt it. I have stopped more than once within two blocks of the place and prayed for strength before I dared go on. The presence of the Lord was so real.

Presumptuous men would sometimes come among us. Especially preachers who would try to spread themselves, in self-opinionation. But their effort was short lived. The breath would be taken from the throne. #16

What happened because of the Azusa Street Revival has fascinated church historians for decades and has yet to be fully understood and explained. The Azusa Street Apostolic Faith Mission used to conduct three services a day, seven days a week, for three and a half years. Thousands of seekers received the baptism in the Holy Spirit with tongues.

The Apostolic Faith, a newspaper Seymour sent free of charge to some 50,000 subscribers, spread word of the revival. From Azusa Street, Pentecostalism spread rapidly around the world and started to become a major force in Christendom.

Blacks and Whites Worshipping

A striking exception to the racism and segregation of the times was the interracial aspects of Azusa Street. The phenomenon of blacks and whites worshipping together under a black pastor seemed incredible to many observers.

William Seymour's place as an important religious figure in the 20th century now seems assured. As early as 1972, Sidney Ahlstrom, the noted church historian from Yale University, said that Seymour was the *"most influential black leader in American religious history."*

Seymour, along with Parham, could well be called the *"co-founders"* of world Pentecostalism.

PART ONE

THE PENTECOSTAL ORIGIN

References

1) Liardon, Roberts. God's Generals. Copyright 1996. Published by Albury Publishing. Printed in Tulsa Oklahoma USA. p79

2) God's Generals. p80

3) God's Generals. p82-83

4) God's Generals. p86

5) Goodrich, Arthur. The Story of the Welsh Revival. Copyright 1905. Published by Fleming H. Revell Company. Printed in New York USA.

6) God's Generals. p89

7) Evans, Eifion. The Welsh Revival of 1904. Copyright 1969. Published by Evangelical Press. Printed in London.

8) Morgan, Vyrnwy. The Welsh Religious Revival 1904-5: A Retrospect and a Criticism. Copyright 1909. Published by Chapman and Hall. Printed in London.

9) Whittaker, Colin. Great Revivals. Copyright 1984. Published by Marshall Pickering. Printed in London. p89

10) God's Generals. p93-94

11) God's Generals. p96-97

12) Bernal, Dick. When Lucifer and Jezebel Join Your Church. Copyright 1994. Published by Jubilee Christian Centre. Printed in San Jose, California USA. p15-18

13) God's Generals. p101

14)   Dixon, Patrick. Signs of Revival. Copyright 1995. Published by Kingsway Publications. Printed in Eastbourne, UK. p171-172

15)   Sumrall, Lester. Pioneers of Faith. Copyright 1995. Published by Harrison House Inc. Printed in Tulsa Oklahoma, USA. p91-96

16)   Signs of Revival. p173-174

Part Two

MISSIONARIES
TAKE PENTECOSTAL POWER

❖

CHAPTER 4

Journeyed Throughout

T he first wave of Azusa pilgrims journeyed throughout the United States spreading the Pentecostal fire primarily in Holiness churches, missions and camp meetings.

Many American Pentecostal pioneers who received tongues at Azusa Street went back to their homes to spread the Movement among their own people. One of the firsts was Gaston Barnabas Cashwell of North Carolina, who first spoke in tongues in 1906.

Under his ministry Cashwell saw several Holiness denominations swept into the new Movement. Also in 1906, Charles Harrison Mason journeyed to Azusa Street and returned to Memphis, Tennessee, to spread the Pentecostal fire in COGIC. Mason and the church he founded were made up of African Americans only one generation removed from slavery. Both Seymour's and Mason's parents had been born as Southern slaves.

Although the church split over the question of tongues in 1907, COGIC experienced such explosive growth that today it is by far the largest Pentecostal denomination in North America, claiming some six million members in 15,300 local churches.

Gradual Progression Sanctification

Another Azusa pilgrim was William H. Durham of Chicago. After receiving tongues at Azusa Street in 1907, he returned to Chicago where he led thousands of Mid Westerners and Canadians into the Pentecostal Movement. His *"finished work"* theology of gradual progression sanctification, which he announced in 1910, led to the formation of the Assemblies of God *(AG)* in 1914.

E.N. Bell and Joseph Flower led the AG. Because many white pastors had been part of Mason's church, when they left to join the AG, the departure was seen partly as a racial separation. In time, the AG was destined to become the largest Pentecostal denomination in the world, claiming by 1995 more than two million US members and some 35 million adherents to 150 countries.

In 1916, a major controversy within the denomination led to the non-Trinitarian *"Oneness"* Pentecostal Movement. This belief taught that Jesus was the only person in the Godhead and that the terms *"Father," "Son,"* and *"Holy Spirit"* were titles.

The Movement leaders Frank Ewart and Glen Cook taught that the only valid water baptism was immersion *"in Jesus' name"* and that speaking in tongues was necessary for salvation. Churches that issued from this Movement included the Pentecostal Assemblies of the World and the United Pentecostal Church.

From New York to Europe

In addition to the ministers who received their Pentecostal experience at Azusa Street, thousands of others were indirectly influenced by the revival in Los Angeles. Among them was Thomas Ball Barratt of Norway, a Methodist pastor who became known as the Pentecostal apostle to Northern and Western Europe.

The late Lester Sumrall *(Dr.)* said in his book ***Pioneers of Faith*** that when I visited T.B Barratt in Norway for a two-week revival in his church, when he was not quite seventy years of age. I first saw Barratt when he met Howard Carter and me at the railroad station in Oslo, the capitol of Norway. He was elegantly dressed, wearing a black hat and black topcoat. He was handsome, thin and tall. His church elders also met us and welcomed us to preach in the Filadelfia Church.

During the time we were holding a meeting there, he told me how he received the infilling of the Holy Spirit and how that transformed his total being, his ministry, and his destiny. He said that it happened when he came to the United States in 1906, although his purpose in visiting this country was to raise funds for the Methodist church, not because he had heard of any new move of God.

However, someone asked him while he was in New York, *"Did you know there is a revival going on in this country?"* When he found out what was happening in California, he wrote to the mission at *Azusa Street* and asked how to receive the same blessing they had received from God. Their response was for him to tarry and wait on God, seeking the baptism of the Spirit daily. Also, they promised to pray for him.

He followed their suggestion, and on October 7, 1906, he received the baptism in the Holy Spirit – which marked the beginning of the Pentecostal Movement in New York.

Barratt, of course, took his new experience to the closest church, which happened to be a street mission. He spoke in tongues that night at the meeting, when he asked a group of people to pray for him.

Some saw *a crown of fire over his head* and what looked like a cloven tongue of fire at the front of the crown. Barratt said he must have spoken in seven or eight different languages that night. As a man who knew languages, he recognised the *"sounds"* of changing from one language to another. Then he sang in another language. The meeting lasted until four A.M.

A man named Robert A. Brown, destined to become another of the pioneers, was at this meeting, so the spark of Holy Spirit fire moved across this continent and soon was taken to Europe. Barratt went back to Norway, called the Methodist clergy together, and said, *"Brethren, I've got it."* They thought he had received a lot of money and asked, *"How much did you get?"*

He replied, *"All I could hold."*

When they said, *"Tell us how much it is,"* he opened to the second chapter of Acts and said, *"I've got it. I speak in tongues."* The Bishop stood up and said, *"Well, you didn't get it here,"* and Barratt was removed from the list of clergy!

However, he did not leave the Methodist Church for some years, and then, it was by his own resignation. That did not stop him. He began to lay hands on people, who received the Holy Spirit by the hundreds. Revival broke out in Christiana, where he pastored a church, in meetings that were packed to standing room only. Many ministers came from all over Europe to see the phenomenon.

Alexander A. Boddy

Among them was an Episcopal pastor named Alexander A. Boddy of Sunderland, England, who visited but did not receive. However, when he went home and preached the new message, others were filled with the Spirit – and the move of God began to move in the British Isles. England had refused to receive from the Welsh Revival a few years before, but this time many received the Holy Spirit.

Boddy eventually received the Holy Spirit for himself. For years Pastor Boddy's church was the centre of the move of the Holy Spirit in Great Britain. His church was like the hub of a wheel with spokes radiating out from it.

This move touched the life of Smith Wigglesworth who knew nothing about the Holy Spirit before meeting Boddy. Smith Wigglesworth and his wife then changed the world.

In our generation, few men touched the world with such remarkable faith as Smith Wigglesworth *(see Chapter Six)*.

Barratt began to take the message of the baptism of the Holy Spirit to other centres in Norway.

Barratt was so full of excitement over the baptism of the Holy Spirit that he could not contain himself. He went into Sweden where a young Baptist preacher just struggling along heard of the great revivals in Oslo. #1

Stockholm, Sweden

Lewi Pethrus *(1884-1974)* visited Barratt's church and received the Holy Spirit. Then Pethrus built one of the largest Pentecostal churches in the world in Stockholm, Sweden.

Pethrus determined the priorities of the Swedish Pentecostal Movement and represented it to the international Movement. He tolerated no competition to his leadership, while he founded a rescue mission, a publishing house, a bible school, a secondary school, a savings bank, and a worldwide radio network that reaches ninety countries and all the continents of the world. He instituted follow-up work, such as correspondence courses, for radio listeners in an effort to tie them into the church.

Pethrus also was a prolific author. His first book, *Jesus Kommer (Jesus is Coming)*, was written in 1912 and is being translated into English by his son, Ingemar. This was followed by a ten-volume series on spiritual subjects, a five-volume series of memoirs, plus other books written after 1956. He also contributed many articles to periodicals.

Other ministry outreaches begun by Pethrus and motivated by his compassion for people, included high schools, relief agencies such as rehabilitation centres for drug addicts and alcoholics, small industries for patients, and special education opportunities. Pethrus also hosted the 1939 World Pentecostal Conference with twenty nations represented. #2

Freelance Revivalist

From 1907 to 1916 Barratt was also a free lance revivalist and prolific author. He published a Christian periodical in Swedish, Finnish, German, Russian and Spanish, as well as Norwegian. He founded Filadelfia Church in Oslo, which became the largest church in Norway with more than three thousand people. He pastored that church until his death, and it is still operating today. However, it has not moved with the outpourings of the following moves of God: the Healing, Charismatic, or Word of Faith Movements. Instead, it has stayed with its beginning Pentecostal revelation.

Dr. Sumrall says, the first thing that really excited him about Barratt was his piano playing. In his church he had two great pianos on the platform. His piano faced toward the pulpit, while the other instrument was placed with the rest of the musicians.

During a service, he would talk awhile, then suddenly sit down at the piano and play and sing. He was an artist of concert calibre, and I loved to hear him. I will never forget Barratt's musicianship. He would ripple arpeggios from one end of the keyboard to the other and sing some of the sweetest melodies I ever heard.

I had never known another pastor who could play the piano so magnificently as well as sing. He was an unusual servant of God, doing an unusual work for God. #3

A Good and Faithful Servant

Thomas Ball Barratt was born in Albaston, Cornwall, on July 22, 1862. His father, a miner, immigrated to Norway in 1867. Barratt's parents and his grandfather, Captain George Ball, were faithful John Wesley Methodists.

His mother was converted at the age of eighteen after praying for two hours, determined to know that she was saved. His father was saved when he was twenty. His family was very well known in their community, both in religious circles and politically.

Both parents loved God with all their hearts, and built churches, they also held meetings in their homes in England and in Norway, after they moved there. Their move came when T.B.'s father was offered the position of manager of mines for his company in Norway.

Barratt felt God's hand upon his life when he was about nine years old, but he did not accept Jesus as Saviour until he was twelve. He believed God had influenced his parents in their decision to choose Norway instead of a similar position in Spain, because his life would have taken a different path otherwise.

At the age of eleven, he returned to England for a formal education, and then later attended Wesleyan College at Taunton, Somerset. At Taunton, a friend led him to

Christ, and a year later, a revival broke out at which about two hundred students were saved, as well as numbers of townspeople.

He returned home to Norway in 1878, where he studied art with a well-known artist and music with Edvard Grieg. The same year he started a Sunday school in his home for people who worked in the mines.

In addition to his parents, he was influenced by the sermons of John Wesley and Dwight L. Moody. When he was seventeen, he read one of Moody's sermons out loud at a women's meeting his mother was hosting, and then prayed. Many at the meeting came forward for salvation.

At eighteen years of age, Barratt prepared his first sermon, after spending time in playing religious music, quiet study, and prayer. His journal notes indicate that he went up on top of a high mountain and preached this sermon to the winds.

Active in Preaching Salvation

Barratt also became active in preaching salvation in the mines where he served as his father's assistant. During this same year, Barratt shared his first extemporaneous sermon. Moody's sermons continued to serve as a foundation to what he taught, but he had no definite plans to become a preacher. He planned to be either a musician or an artist.

However, in 1882, when he was nearly twenty, Barratt passed an examination at the *Methodist Episcopal Quarterly Conference*, held at Bergen, Norway, to become a *"local preacher."* This was sort of a layman to speak to small groups and churches or to substitute for fully ordained pastors.

About this time, his recreation included translating English books into Norwegian – he spoke both languages fluently – and fighting with a bear. The bear lost, according to reports of the time! Also, he responded in writing to an attack on Methodism written by a pastor of another denomination.

Methodism at that time was still almost as controversial in some countries as Pentecostalism has been in the twentieth century. As I said, those spiritual giants who pioneered the *"latter rain"* of the Holy Spirit had to be rugged individuals.

Choose Ye This Day Whom Ye Will Serve

In January 1884, he preached a message entitled *"Choose Ye This Day Whom Ye Will Serve,"* which triggered a revival that went for weeks on the mountain where they lived.

He married Laura Jakobsen in May 1887, and began to pastor a church at Christiana, where their first child was born. Barratt was ordained a deacon in 1889, and in 1891, he became an elder in the Methodist Episcopal Church of Norway. After that, he pastored several churches.

By his thirty-seventh birthday, this artist-musician who had no plans to preach, had held more than five thousand meetings.

In 1902 he founded the Oslo City Mission, in 1904 he became the editor of its paper, *Byposten*. Both his parents had died by this time, but they must have been proud of him long before they died.

Barratt went into Sweden, Switzerland, England, Holland, and even into India with the message of the **Baptism of the Holy Spirit.** Thus Barratt not only founded the Norwegian Pentecostal Movement but also became a key figure in the establishment of Pentecostal churches throughout Europe.

Barratt took the knowledge of the baptism of the Holy Spirit from America to leading preachers in Europe, when he could have returned to Norway and buried it. Everywhere he went he planted the blessing of Pentecost.

Directly or indirectly, he touched the lives of many other spiritual pioneers. #4

❖

CHAPTER 5

Chicago to Chile

Also hailing form Chicago was Willis C. Hoover, the Methodist missionary to Chile who in 1909 led a Pentecostal revival in the Chilean Methodist Episcopal Church. After being excommunicated from the Methodist Episcopal Church, Hoover and 37 of his followers organised the Pentecostal Methodist Church, which has some 1.5 million adherents in Chile.

Born on July 20, *(1856-1936)*, in Freeport, Illinois, to Methodist parents, Willis Collins Hoover pursued the professions of medicine and architecture. In 1884, he repeatedly received what he called a strong inner impression, *"South…America, South…America, South…America."*

When Hoover realised God was calling him to the mission fields of South America, he told the Lord he would go as soon as he paid his debts and found a wife. In 1888, Hoover married.

Hoover went to Chile as a Methodist missionary, received the baptism of the Holy Spirit and founded the Pentecostal Movement in Chile. He raised up one of the largest evangelical groups in Latin America.

Although he had no formal training in theology, he gained an appointment in 1889 as rector of the Iquique English School in Northern Chile under the quasi-independent mission of Methodist bishop, William Taylor.

From serving a small Spanish-speaking congregation in Iquique, Hoover was promoted to superintendent of the Iquique District when Chile was divided into three areas in 1897 and appointed pastor in Valparaiso, the largest church in the conference in 1902.

Kept up with the Activities

Hoover expanded his evangelistic thrust to include branch chapels, class meetings, house-to-house visitation and cottage meetings. He kept up with the activities going on in the Church worldwide as much as possible. He read about Evan Roberts *(1878-1951)* in Wales and A.B. Simpson *(1843-1919)* in the United States.

He learned of the Pentecostal outpouring in India through the book of his wife's former classmate. *The Baptism of the Holy Ghost and Fire* by Minnie F. Abrams told of a revival among the widows and orphans in a school and home operated by a high class Indian where Miss Abrams was then working.

After reading this book, Hoover asked others about the Pentecostal outpouring, which with the exception of tongues differed little from the emotional expression of pioneer Methodism. It was during this time that Hoover and his wife also heard from a friend in Oak Park, Illinois, who had experienced the baptism of the Holy Spirit with the evidence of speaking in other tongues.

Hoover's Pentecostal activities and those of Nellie Laidlaw, a new convert and prophetess he had endorsed, cost him the superintendency but not his pulpit at the 1910 conference in Valparaiso. However, effective May 1, Hoover resigned from the ministry and membership of the Methodist Episcopal Church, taking most of his own and two other congregations with him. He reorganised his congregation into what he called *"Iglesia Methodista Nacional,"* which experienced extensive growth.

Iglesia Evangelica Pentecostal de Chile

When this Movement split in 1932, Hoover established the Iglesia Evangelica Pentecostal de Chile, which he headed until his death four years later.

When Hoover built his first church in Chile, which would seat twelve hundred, his congregation at that time numbered less than five hundred. He often prayed, *"Lord, do not let this building mock us. We are building it to save sinners. Thou must fill it,"* according to his own writings.

Hoover's work was not without opposition from Christians and co-labourers as well as unbelievers.

Newspaper headlines called him *"The Great Impostor,"* *"hypnotist"* and *"suggestionist."* The public slander against the baptism of the Holy Spirit was severe, so he knew this persecution was not personal but for the Word's sake.

In the year following Hoover's separation from the Methodist Episcopal Church, his congregation added one hundred and fifty new members. Board members and some congregational members left Hoover's church to begin new works, thus multiplying Hoover's influence.

Not only were people being baptised in the Holy Spirit but also supernatural healings were taking place. People were healed from smallpox and delivered from insanity, for example. However, Hoover's primary focus remained on the transformation of lives.

Tried and tested on the mission field, Hoover and his wife became ill with typhoid fever. Also, they went through a smallpox epidemic where fifty to one hundred people died daily, and they lived through an earthquake, but Mrs. Hoover was able to rush home from a prayer meeting and get their children outside just before the roof fell in.

Hoover translated hundreds of hymns into Spanish, which are still in use today. He was an apostle of Pentecost to an entire nation. #5

African Pentecostalism from Zion

African Pentecostalism owes its origins to the work of John Graham Lake *(1870-1935)*, who began his ministry as a Methodist preacher but who later prospered in business as an insurance executive. In 1898 his wife was miraculously healed of tuberculosis under the ministry of Alexander Dowie, founder of the religious community called Zion City near Chicago.

Doctor John Alexander Dowie was born in Scotland in 1847. When he was thirteen, Dowie and his parents moved to Australia. He first experienced the healing power of God at the age of sixteen, when the Lord healed him. Dowie had a strong and dominant personality, and was a man with strong determination. Once he set his mind on doing something, he went ahead and did it.

At the age of twenty-one Dowie came to a point in his life where he made a positive decision to serve the Lord and to fulfil the call upon his life. During his short working life he had saved some money, which helped him to begin his studies to prepare for the ministry. Within two years he enrolled in Edinburgh University to study in the Free Church School, majoring in theology and political science. It is said that Dowie had an incredible hunger and thirst for the Word of God, enhanced by his photographic memory.

Back in Australia

Some time later during his studies he received a telegram from his father in Australia requesting his return because of the family business affairs and the desire for the young Dowie to take on the families business. On returning Dowie informed his father that he did not wish for any inheritance within the family business because of his love for the ministry and the pull of God within his heart to full time ministry.

Now back in Australia, an invitation came requesting that he would pastor a congregational church in Alma, which he accepted, but as time went on he began to long for bigger congregations. In 1875 Dowie moved again to a large group in Newton, a suburb of Sydney.

While pastoring in Newton, Dowie's church suffered great loss during a plague, when forty of his members died. This really disturbed him and he began to seek God, during which time Dowie received great revelation concerning healing. Soon after receiving this revelation he received an urgent call to pray for a dying young girl, who having once received prayer from Dowie was healed instantly of her deathly fever and sat up in bed to eat! Others were also healed and from that time onwards, not another person in his church died as a result of that plague.

Dowie then built a large temple, which seated 20,000 people. Right from the beginning of his ministry the masses followed him. He was well known for his audacity and boldness and preached strongly against alcohol and drinking which did not make him popular with organised crime! His preaching shut down saloons with those getting saved no longer wanting to drink, and others prayed against and boycotted the saloons.

Great prayer and Sensitivity

Dowie was a man of great prayer and sensitivity to the *Holy Spirit* and one day he was in his office writing when he felt the Holy Spirit tell him several times to get up, leave the office and go for a walk. As he was beginning his journey, the office blew up! A bomb had been planted there to kill him.

He moved to Chicago USA, *(1888)* and here his ministry really took off. He built a healing room where many miracles happened. Some people in Chicago got mad at him and tried to remove him but instead God removed them! He went on and built a City, which he called ***"Zion Illinois,"*** this being the greatest venture he ever took on and within two years it had 10,000 citizens and was very successful.

However, Dowie went from a life of prayer, to doing 48-hour stretches, working in the city. Because Dowie left his prayer closet and stress managed to take hold of him, he began to claim that he was ***"Elijah come back from the dead."*** This was his downfall and men of God from all over the world began to discredit him.

His ministry began to collapse and by the time **he preached his last sermon only 400 people were left in his audience.** Dowie had been a man of great discernment and prophecy and God used him mightily in his former days but sadly, through neglect of his prayer life, his great ministry fell, and in 1907 he died in his wheelchair.

John Alexander Dowie went down in history as an impostor, yet he was a genius called of God. Even in the midst of his error, **he prophesied the coming of radio and television to our generation.** He had his failures, but from his influence came many great men of God.

His ministry produced John G. Lake, the great apostle to South Africa; F. F. Bosworth, and his brother B. B. Bosworth, whose healing campaigns touched untold millions; Gordon Lindsay, whose life and ministry resulted in the great interdenominational college, **"Christ for the Nations,"** in Dallas, Texas; Raymond T. Richey, healing crusader; and Charles Parham, *"The Father of Pentecost,"* whose bible school in Topeka, Kansas, ushered in another move of the Holy Spirit. Many more had large radio ministries and powerful mission works.

Without a doubt, John Alexander Dowie succeeded in making the bible alive to untold millions. He was an instrument used of God to restore the keys of divine healing and the revelation of repentance to a lukewarm, lethargic generation.

If there is a moral to the message of the failure in his life, that message is this: Never sway from what God has commanded you to do in the earth. No matter what your age, your generation has not passed until you exit the earth and enter heaven. So if God has commanded you to fulfil a commission, make it your utmost priority as long as you live. #6

Lake influenced by Dowie went to Africa

In 1907, John G. Lake was baptised in the Holy Spirit and spoke in tongues. *(Zion City also produced almost 500 preachers who entered the ranks of the Pentecostal Movement.)*

After his Pentecostal experience, Lake abandoned the insurance business to answer a long-standing call to minister in South Africa. In April 1908, he led a large missionary party to Johannesburg where he began to spread the Pentecostal message throughout the nation.

Lake succeeded in founding two large and influential Pentecostal churches in South Africa. The white branch took the name *Apostolic Faith Mission* in 1910, borrowing from the name of the famous mission on Azusa Street. David du Plessis, known to the world as "Mr. Pentecost," came from this church. The black branch eventually developed into the *Zion Christian Church*, which had six million members by 1993.

Soon after Lake returned to the United States, the Movement reached the Slavic world through the ministry of a Russian-born Baptist pastor Ivan Voronaev, who received the Pentecostal experience in New York City in 1919. Through prophecies, he was led to take his family with him to Odessa, Ukraine in 1922. There he established the first Pentecostal church in the Soviet Union. Voronaev was arrested, imprisoned and martyred in a communist prison in 1943. The churches he founded survived extreme persecution and have become today a major religious force in Russia and the former Soviet Union.

Pentecostalism reached Korea

Pentecostalism reached Korea through the ministry of Mary Rumsey, an American missionary who had been baptised in the Holy Spirit at Azusa Street in 1907. At that time, Rumsey believed that she was called to Japan and Korea. It was not until 1928, however, that she landed in Korea. Before World War II, she had planted eight Pentecostal churches there before being forced out of the country by the Japanese.

In 1952, those eight churches were turned over to the AG, whose missionaries immediately opened a bible school in Seoul.

One of the first students to enrol was a young convert by the name of **Paul Yonggi Cho.** After he graduated from bible college, Cho pioneered a Korean church that became the Yoido Full Gospel church. The Church today claims some 700,000 members, the largest single Christian congregation in the world.

His story began in 1954, a staunch young Buddhist lay dying of tuberculosis, having been given only some three months to live by the doctors. Through the visits and faithful witness of a young Christian girl he eventually surrendered his life to Christ. The tears of that eighteen-year-old girl deeply moved him as she pleaded with him to receive Christ. She left him with her bible, which he read and not only was he gloriously converted but within a short time he was healed.

Within a few years he completed bible school training and began to pastor a tent church in a slum area of Seoul. Today his name is known around the world as the pastor of the largest church in the world.

The tent was just an old American Marine tent and it leaked badly when it rained! Yonggi Cho says, "Those were days of struggle. When it rained, we had to place buckets in strategic places to catch the leaks that would trickle through the hand sown tent roof. My congregation was poor and their lives were empty of everything except problems.

The days in the tent church were often days of discouragement." There were several times he packed his bags and was ready to get on a train and leave. But he stuck it out and God taught him the great principles of faith, which have made him one of the most significant Christian leaders in the world today.

In that humble tent people with all kinds of diseases and problems were healed and helped. Gradually the congregation began to increase and they moved down town to the West Gate area of Seoul. They then had some six hundred members. In 1972 Billy Graham was the first to preach in the magnificent new building in Yoido, the government district of Seoul.

The Full Gospel Central Church

The Central Church when first erected was capable of seating 10,000. Since then it has been further enlarged to accommodate the ever-increasing membership. On 31st May 1981 it had 177,489 adult members, all active participants in the 12,421 home cells. Before the end of 1981 the membership reached 200,000. #7

The secret of the success of the ever-growing church in Seoul is prayer, and prayer with fasting. In 1973 Paul Yonggi Cho established what is called their Prayer Mountain, which is situated 45km north of Seoul, it is placed strategically between the Capital of South Korea and the border with North Korea.

The person behind this great concept of prayer is Sister Jashil Choi who is committed to prayer and fasting. Jashil Choi is Yonggi Cho's mother-in-law; she started making nightly trips to the mountain at Osanri to pray for the needs of the church and its members.

Since she started this in 1973 the whole church has caught the vision. People there are praying and fasting all the time and visitors testify to being immediately conscious of the presence of God. The prayer mountain is renowned for miracles: they are happening all the time. Above all they pray for worldwide revival. The church in Seoul conducts several church services each Sunday each one attended by well over 20,000 people.

Yonggi Cho says *"It has been historically true that prayer has been the key to every revival in the history of Christianity."* *"No man can schedule a revival."* He also says "For God alone is the giver of life, but…when the *'fullness of time'* has come and prayer ascends from a few earnest hearts, then history teaches it is time for the tide of revival to sweep in once more."

From Chicago, the Influence of William Durham

The Movement of the Pentecostal Experience spread quickly in those early years to Italy and South America. Two Italian immigrants from Chicago, Luigi Francescon and Giacomo Lombardi founded thriving Italian Pentecostal Movements after 1908 in the United States, Brazil, Argentina and Italy.

Argentina has witnessed episodes worthy of the Acts of the Apostles. As in Brazil, the Pentecostal work was started by these two humble, "unknown" believers, newly-filled with the Spirit of God, who at the call of God went from Chicago to Buenos Aires and arrived unheralded. From that humble beginning there are now hundreds of Christian assemblies in various parts of Argentina. #8

Also in 1952 in Tallahassee, Florida, a forty-four year old evangelist, Tommy Hicks, was in prayer when God gave him a vision of a map of South America. The map was covered with a vast field of yellow grain, ready for harvest. It was a clear Macedonian call. As he prayed the grain changed to men and women with uplifted hands crying, ***"Come, Brother Hicks, come and help us!"***

As he continued to pray God gave him a message which he wrote in his bible:

"For two snows will not pass over the earth until thou shalt go to this land, for thou shalt not go by boat nor by land but as a bird, flying through the air shalt thou go."

Hicks kept the vision to himself and the message. But three months later in California in a pastor's home, during prayer the pastor's wife stretched out her hand and repeated the identical message.

Tommy Hicks began to prepare for the journey, knowing virtually nothing about Argentina. God provided funds for a one-way ticket to Buenos Aires. During the last part of the flight the name *"Peron"* kept coming to his mind. He felt sure God was speaking but the name meant nothing to him, so he asked the stewardess who told him, *"Mr. Peron is the President of Argentina."* Hicks took it that God wanted him to talk to the President, so he sought an interview with him.

All the missionaries warned him against even trying; Peron was a dictator and freedom was limited. It could be dangerous. Hicks, however, would not be deterred. He presented himself at the office of the Minister of Religion – *"No, Peron would not see him."*

Then the Minister's secretary came in limping; his left leg was stiffened and black. Hicks suggested they prayed about it and the secretary scoffed that even Christ himself couldn't help his leg!

Nevertheless, Hicks prayed and God worked a miracle. The astonished and delighted secretary forthwith promised to take Hicks to see Peron. The way having been so marvellously prepared, Peron was more than responsive and gave instructions that help be given to him.

Hicks was given the use of a large stadium and free access to government radio and press. The crusade had a far-reaching effect. Peter Wagner says, "Recent studies on the church in Argentina have revealed the crucial importance of the Tommy Hicks' campaign of 1954, not only for the Pentecostals, but also for all other churches which co-operated."

Note: Charles Peter Wagner, *(born 1930) is a Christian theologian, missiologist, missionary, writer, teacher, and church growth specialist.*

A Sovereign Breakthrough

Arno Enns, who has written the *Standard Church History* of Argentina, calls the Hicks campaign "a sovereign breakthrough of God."

The influential book, *Latin American Church Growth* says, "Many Evangelicals in Argentina, whether or not they agree with Hicks' theology, admit that his meetings broke the back of the rigid Argentine resistance to the evangelical witness."

He preached for fifty-two days to an aggregate attendance of some two million, with an accepted figure of some 200,000 in the final meeting. Researchers seem satisfied that a figure of something approaching 20,000 converts is right, which was the greatest gain ever in Argentina. All Evangelicals profited, but the Pentecostals particularly began a period of rapid growth, which was still continuing in the 1980's. #9

The Brazilian Assemblies

In South Bend, Indiana – near Chicago – two Swedish Baptist immigrants, **Daniel Berg** and **Gunnar Vingren,** received the Pentecostal experience. Believing they were called prophetically to Brazil, they embarked on a missionary trip in 1910 that resulted in the formation of the Brazilian Assemblies of God. The Brazilian Assemblies developed into the largest national Pentecostal Movement in the world and had some 25 million members by 1990.

"Brazil is a land where the greatest national revival of the twentieth century is now in force," says **Steve Durasoff** in *Bright Wind of the Spirit.*

Church growth specialist, Peter Wagner, says "The Protestant Church is increasing at a rate three times that of the population in general.

- In 1900 there were about 50,000 Protestants in Latin America.

- In the 1930's it passed the two million mark.

- In the 1950's it passed the five million mark.

- In the 1960's it passed the 10 million mark.

- In the 1970's it zoomed past the 20 million mark.

- Some statisticians project something around 100 million for 2000 AD." (*Look Out the Pentecostals are Coming.*)

Brazil, with a population around 120 million occupies half of the South American continent. This great and developing country has been experiencing almost continuous revival for over seventy years, and there is no sign of abatement – rather the very opposite. **When Dr. Billy Graham visited Brazil he was asked if he knew the secret of the growth of the work of God there. He replied, *"Every Pentecostal believer is a preacher."***

The commencement of the Pentecostal work in Brazil is one of the great romances of Pentecostal missionary work. In 1910 when the two Swedish immigrants to America, **Daniel Berg** and **Gunnar Vingren,** were called by God to leave Chicago and commence a missionary work in Para, Brazil. This began when they were in a small prayer meeting in South Bend, Indiana, a prophecy was given to them telling them to *"go to Para."* Para? They had never heard of it. Searching in the public library they discovered that it was a state in Brazil. #10

"They arrived in Brazil, bewildered and exhausted," says Peter Wagner. "Their wool suits were hardly appropriate attire for one of the world's hottest tropical cities. They sat on a park bench, not knowing what to do next, but praying for God to guide them. He guided them first to a Methodist missionary, who introduced them to a friendly Baptist pastor who in turn provided them with lodging in some rooms behind the church."

Their red-hot message of the Holy Ghost power, however, proved rather too much for their newfound friends and soon they formed their own church. From the first, God worked with them in revival power and blessing.

Today the proof that they were truly called of God is that the work they started is now the largest Protestant Work in all Latin America. Daniel Berg died in 1963 in his eightieth year, a highly respected leader; his companion Gunner Vingren preceded him in his home-call by a few years; but the work they founded, Assemblies of God in Brazil, is still moving forward in revival power with some ten million members and adherents. #11

❖

CHAPTER 6

Smith Wigglesworth

B ack in England the most prominent and respected evangelists in the twentieth century was **Smith Wigglesworth** *(1859-1947)*. His accomplishments as an evangelist have become legendary, and Wigglesworth remains an inspiration for all believers seeking to experience the miraculous and loving intervention of a caring God.

Saved at the age of eight through the prayers of his Methodist grandmother, young Wigglesworth proceeded to gain his first convert, his own mother. At the age of sixteen, Wigglesworth encountered **William Booth** and the Salvation Army. He was truly an evangelist, bringing hundreds to Christ each month as he simply witnessed to the things of God's Word and His plan of salvation.

He and his wife, Polly, whom he met while working with the Salvation Army, never considered that their ministry might extend beyond the borders of their community of Bradford, England. Polly, who's given name was Mary Jane, preached, and Wigglesworth met new believers at the altar and led them in professions of faith. He was a true soul-winner.

In 1907, however, Wigglesworth was baptised in the Holy Spirit at Sunderland, England, under the ministry of **Alexander and Mary Boddy,** who had been part of the Welsh revival.

Of special interest to the British people is the little group that gathered around the godly vicar of **All Saints' Parish Church, Sunderland. Alexander A. Boddy** had been their spiritual leader since 1886. When the Revival broke out in Wales in 1904 he made a special journey to Wales, and stood beside Evan Roberts in the midst of some of the amazing scenes of Tonypandy.

When he recounted to his people at All Saints what he had personally seen in Wales, it stirred both pastor and people up to yet more earnest prayer and expectation of great things from God. Sunderland was being prepared in the purposes of God to become a centre of new and far-reaching blessing. The circumstances were humble enough. The meetings were held in a wooden barn-like structure now pulled down. #12

Associated Holiness with Baptism

Smith in his thinking at that time associated holiness with baptism. Although there were Pentecostal teachers who were teaching that this baptism was for power and not holiness, but Wigglesworth would have none of that.

"The Holy Spirit will come when a man is cleansed," were his words, adding, "there must be a purging of the old life. I never saw anyone baptised who was not clean within."

Smith Wigglesworth was now forty-eight. He was a very successful businessman, and his spiritual life was healthy. Bowland Street Mission was thriving, many people were being blessed and it was gaining a reputation for its emphasis on the teaching of holiness and healing. *"We thought that we had got all that was coming to us on spiritual lines,"* he said. However, he continued to be limited in his public ministry. He still found great difficulty in stringing even a few words together let alone sentences.

Polly was always the preacher, though she repeatedly encouraged Smith to share the preaching with her. She would often announce that on the following Sunday her husband would preach the sermon, but such events were invariably accompanied by agonising days for Smith. Then the *"sermons"* would be short-lived and end by Wigglesworth inviting members of the congregation to the pulpit to finish the preaching.

Anglican Church in Sunderland

One day Smith heard of unusual happenings in an Anglican Church in Sunderland. From all accounts, Christians were receiving similar experience to the Early Church as recorded in the Acts of the Apostles. *"Have you heard the latest?"* said a visitor to his home. *"They are receiving the Holy Spirit in Sunderland and speaking in tongues. I have decided to go and see this thing for myself,"* continued the man. *"Would you like to come with me?"* And the man offered to pay Smith's travelling expenses.

Meanwhile back at Sunderland **Alexander Boddy** and a small group of his parishioners continued earnestly in prayer. They had been praying for the last two years, when Boddy heard of *the blessings in Oslo under the ministry of Barratt*. Barratt had recently returned from USA. *(Pastor Barratt was a church leader in Norway.)*

Once again Alexander Boddy travelled in search of accurate information. Early in 1907 he was in Norway, this time alongside the Methodist minister **T. B. Barratt,** witnessing the revival that was taking place.

Returning home he wrote, "My four days in Christiania *[as it was then known – it is now Oslo]* can never be forgotten. I stood with Evan Roberts in Tonypandy, but have never witnessed such scenes as those in Norway." Later that year Boddy published a pamphlet entitled **Pentecostal for England,** which he distributed at the Keswick Convention of 1907. In the pamphlet he wrote, *"It is said that 20,000 people today are speaking in tongues, or have so spoken." (That number today of course is in the Millions.)*

Barratt decided to return to the United States to renew his contacts with the men and women who were now emerging as leaders of the young Pentecostal Movement, *(Azusa Street)*. Hearing of his intentions, Boddy persuaded him to call at Sunderland on route.

Sending a letter of **invitation** and informing him that visitors were already gathering at Sunderland from many parts of England. They had been praying for months that God would send His servant over and that Pentecostal blessing would graciously crown his ministry.

Mr. Barratt records in his journal a deep feeling of his own unworthiness, but a conviction that the call to the land of his fathers was of the Lord, and therefore he set forth in complete dependence upon God. He arrived on Saturday and that evening in Sunderland, they held the first prayer meeting in the vestry *"with great blessing."*

On the next day Pastor Barratt was asked to preach in All Saints' Parish Church immediately following the usual evening service conducted by the vicar. The service was followed by a prayer meeting in the vestry, where *"many received very marked blessings, and a few came through to a scriptural baptism in the Holy Ghost 'for we heard them speak with tongues and magnify God.'"* That meeting continued until 4 am on Monday morning.

Revival in the British Isles

The Pentecostal Revival had commenced in the British Isles. The daily newspapers were used by Divine Providence almost more than any other agency to bring the news of what was happening in Sunderland before the notice of multitudes who otherwise might never have heard. Of course they fastened upon the more spectacular phenomena accompanying the services, particularly the speaking with tongues, but almost without exception the reporters were impartial, and not one paper contained a bitter word.

The extent of these reports probably justified Mr. Barratt's words on September 13th that *"the eyes of the religious millions of Great Britain are now fixed upon Sunderland."* Yet the religious periodicals, as a whole, maintained a frigid silence.

A constant stream of seekers continued to come to Sunderland to see and hear for themselves these scenes of reported Pentecostal blessing and phenomena. Some were critical, and one local minister violently attacked the new Movement that had sprung up with such power in his vicinity. Those were busy days for an already busy parish minister, and the vicarage became a hallowed spot for many visitors.

Destined later to become an outstanding world-wide Pentecostal preacher was **Smith Wigglesworth,** then leader of Bowland Street Mission, Bradford and a master-plumber who *received the baptism of the Holy Spirit with the sign of tongues in All Saints' Vicarage on Tuesday, October 20th, 1907.*

And so it was that this Norwegian Methodist minister, a forerunner of the Pentecostal Movement in Europe, found himself in an Anglican pulpit in September 1907 describing the baptism of the Holy Spirit with the speaking in other tongues.

Though the vicar and his parishioners of All Saints' Parish Church did not realise it at the time, **it was to mark the beginning of the British Pentecostal Movement.**

Four Days that Changed a Life

Smith Wigglesworth was not aware of these remarkable developments as he boarded the train for Sunderland. His Bowland Street mission was experiencing spiritual blessings more than neighbouring churches. Many healings were taking place through his ministry.

Wigglesworth experienced a healing during his early years that God would eventually use to alter his destiny. His ruptured appendix was healed, and Wigglesworth strongly believed that God had endowed him with a special **gift of healing** for those with appendicitis.

Smith believed in different kinds of gifts of faith. For example, he cited **Rees Howells,** founder of the **Bible College of Wales,** as a man of faith for finance, whereas Smith did not claim to have such a gift. **His gift was for healing**. But he also recognised that you had to cultivate faith in God.

However, although he reckoned that he had been baptised in the Holy Spirit *(as taught at the Keswick Convention meetings),* he was not fully satisfied, and when on the platform in his Mission hall he continued to be tongue-tied, leaving Polly to do the preaching. But now that the news of people speaking in tongues in Sunderland – just as they did in the beginning of Christianity – had been given to him, he could not rest until he knew all about it for himself.

On his arrival two former members of his Bradford Mission, now living in Sunderland met him. They did not lose time in warning him against the meetings at All

Saints'. They believed them to be heretical and contrary to the scriptures. Undeterred by this, Smith and his travelling companion decided to attend Mr. Boddy's prayer meeting without delay. And so it was that on Saturday October 25th, just a month after the visit of T. B. Barratt, Wigglesworth found himself in the parish hall of All Saints' Church, Monkwearmouth.

God's blessing was already being experienced in Bradford, and the night before Wigglesworth had left for Sunderland many people had fallen prostrate on the floor under the power of God. In contrast, the All Saints' meeting was *"flat."* He began to wonder why he had come; there did not seem to be as much power as in his Bowland Street Mission. He was disappointed. ***"But I was hungry for God,"*** **said Smith.** And he knew that God was aware of his hunger, however much was to be misunderstood by the others at the "waiting meetings."

Testimony Time

A feature of these early Pentecostal meetings was *"testimony time,"* similar to the Methodist class meetings of Smith's youth. One man who made an impression on Wigglesworth testified to having spoken in tongues after waiting on God for three weeks. Not given to the niceties of behaviour, Smith called out, *"Let's hear those tongues. That's what I came for. Let's hear it." "When you are baptised in the Spirit you will speak in tongues,"* he was told.

Smith Wigglesworth was throughout his whole life nothing if not earnest. He sought more and more of God with his whole heart. So it was that at seven o'clock the next morning, Sunday October 26th, he went to the Salvation Army prayer meeting.

> *"Three times in that prayer meeting I was smitten to the floor by the mighty power of God," he said. "Somewhat ashamed of my position, lest I should be misunderstood, I tried to control myself by sitting up again and kneeling and praying."*

Wigglesworth had an experience that morning similar to the one described by Daniel 10; he *"continued with the Holy Spirit glow all the day still realising a mightier work to follow."*

Later that day, now at All Saints', he attended Holy Communion followed by the *"waiting meetings"* which were arranged for those seeking the Pentecostal baptism. His hunger for God continued to increase and he continued in prayer throughout Monday October 27th.

At about eleven o'clock on the Tuesday morning October 28th, he was on his knees in the vicarage when,

> *"The fire fell and burned in me until the Holy Spirit revealed absolute purity before God... My whole being became full of light and holy presence, and in the revelation I saw an empty cross. At the same time I could see the Jesus I loved and adored, crowned in the glory in a reigning position."*

For four days Smith had wanted nothing but God. But he now began to feel the pressure of his business back home. With some reluctance he came to the decision that he had to return home even though he had not received the Pentecostal baptism and spoken in tongues.

He told Mrs. Boddy, the vicar's wife, of his decision, concluding, *"I'm going away, but I've not received the tongues yet."* *"It's not tongues you need,"* replied the woman wisely, ***"it's the baptism."*** He protested that he had already received his baptism some years before, in July 1893 to be precise. Then, as he was about to leave, he added that he would still be glad to have her lay hands on him.

The Fire of the Holy Spirit

This gracious and godly lady agreed to pray for him there in the vicarage. As she did so he felt the ***Fire-Power of the Holy Spirit*** lay hold on him as never before. Mrs. Boddy left the room and Wigglesworth remained alone, *"bathed in the power of God."* ***"I was conscious of the cleansing of the precious blood and I cried out in a new-found ecstasy, 'Clean! Clean! Clean!'"*** He was filled with an increased consciousness of cleansing. Then he began to speak in languages unknown to him. His whole being was enveloped with an unusual feeling as waves of worship began to roll over him.

So intense was the sense of God's presence that he remained there, unable to move, praising and glorifying his Saviour for a long time.

> *"I began to praise him in other tongues as the Spirit gave me utterance,"* he later told his wife. *"I could no longer speak in English. Then I knew that though **I had previously received anointings, now I had received the baptism in the Holy Spirit as they did on the day of Pentecost.**"*

When recalling these events he would say, *"Today I am actually living in the Acts of the Apostles' time,"* with the qualification that, *"the moment you pass through the Acts of the Apostles you are ready for the Epistles."*

The Epistles are written for Baptised Believers

Immediately after his baptism he returned to the meeting which was then in progress and interrupted the vicar who was on his feet speaking. Smith asked if he could speak. Alexander Boddy agreed to this unusual request, promptly took his seat and allowed Wigglesworth to address the meeting.

The effect was dramatic. Though previously he had never been able to hold the attention of any congregation for the briefest of periods, now those in the meeting gave him rapt attention as he spoke with great conviction.

When he had finished, a man stood to his feet and said, *"We have been rebuking this man because he was so intensely hungry, but he has come to us for a few days and has received the baptism. And some of us have been waiting here for weeks and have not received."*

This stirred the congregation to the extent that within a short time fifty of those present were filled with the Holy Spirit and spoke in other tongues.

Doubts Defeated and a Challenge Issued

Smith Wigglesworth's next move was equally dramatic. He sent a telegram to Polly which said, ***"I have received*** *the baptism in the Holy Ghost and have spoken in other tongues."* But during the train journey home the devil began to torment him, *"Are you going to take this thing to Bradford?"* The way he felt just at that moment was that he had nothing to take, and he began to question the rashness of sending the telegram to his wife.

However, he soon checked himself. He had always said that you should rely on your faith in God and not your own feelings. So, in his customary if somewhat unique style, and to the astonishment of his fellow travellers in the railway coach, he shouted aloud, *"Yes, I'm taking it!"*

Wigglesworth Speaking in Tongues

His son George was waiting for him when he arrived at Bradford's railway station. *"Father, have you been speaking in tongues?"* *"Yes, George,"* replied Wigglesworth. *"Then let's hear you,"* said George. But Smith said nothing; he did not even try. He was always strongly opposed to invitations to speak in tongues as a demonstration, and later condemned such practices as *"activities of the 'flesh.'"*

Father and son made their way home to find mother, waiting for them. Polly could be as direct with her words as Smith. As he stepped inside their home she looked him up and down with a calculated gaze. *"So you've been speaking in tongues, have you?"* she said somewhat scornfully. In a subdued voice he responded, *"Well, er...yes."* *"Well, I want you to understand,"* said his wife rather firmly, *"I am as much baptised as you are, and I don't speak in tongues."*

Then pushing the knife in a little further, she added, *"I've been preaching for more than twenty years and you have sat beside me on the platform tongue-tied. But on Sunday you'll preach yourself my man, and I'll be there to see what there is in it."* That said, she walked out of the room, leaving a very thoughtful, and perhaps a little shaken, Smith Wigglesworth.

What's happened to the Man?

Polly Wigglesworth kept her word. On the following Sunday she took her seat on one of the long benches at the back of the mission hall alongside a young woman, called Florence Tear, who was to become Polly's daughter-in-law, the wife of Seth and mother of Leslie. "It was a remarkable event. Father Wigglesworth was always neatly and cleanly dressed. He used to sit on the platform but never preach," she said.

Smith walked the length of the hall and, with a small bible in his hand, ascended the three short steps to the platform. As he walked towards the front of the hall he did not know what he was going to say in his sermon. But as he ascended the platform steps God spoke to him. He was told to begin with the words in Isaiah 61:

"The Spirit of the Lord God is upon me, because the Lord has anointed me to bring good tidings to the afflicted; he has sent me to bind up the broken-hearted, to proclaim liberty to the captives, and the opening of the prison to those who are bound."

Then he began to preach. Soon he felt the mighty power of God surge through him, and though he had a limited vocabulary, words rushed out of him like a torrent of water. Previously when he had attempted to preach he had always broken down weeping, but now he was fluent. Furthermore, he marched around the platform, fully at ease like a seasoned speaker.

Polly sat at the back of the hall. She was completely astounded and could hardly believe her ears, let alone her eyes. She could not keep still. As Smith continued with his preaching so Polly kept moving, from one part of the bench to another, and then another, talking to herself, *"That's not my Smith. That's not my Smith."* Then she would add, *"Amazing, amazing,"* and **"What's happened to the man?"** And that's how she continued throughout his sermon, unable to keep still and sitting on every part of that long bench at the back of Bowland Street Mission hall.

Polly watched this uneducated and previously fumbling, stumbling plumber of the Yorkshire Dales, her much loved Smith, speaking not only coherently but with a force that would have been the envy of many a politician. Later he said,

"Suddenly I felt that I had prophetic utterances, which were flowing like a river by the power of the Holy Spirit."

As Smith Wigglesworth stood to announce the closing hymn the secretary of the mission rose to his feet and said to the congregation, **"I want what our leader has received."** But as he went to sit down he missed his seat and fell lengthwise on the floor. Then Seth Wigglesworth, Smith's eldest son, stood up and said that he also wanted what his father had experienced, but when he tried to sit down he missed his seat and he too went sprawling along the floor.

A further eleven members of that congregation did the same. *"The strangest thing,"* recounted Wigglesworth, *"was that they were all laughing in the Spirit, and laughing at each other. The Lord had really turned again this captivity of Zion, and the mouths of his children were being filled with laughter according to the Word of the Lord in Psalm 126."*

That was the beginning of the Pentecostal Movement in Bradford, with many hundreds receiving the baptism in the Holy Spirit accompanied by the gift of tongues. #13

Wigglesworth the Preacher

If you did not have the privilege of hearing Smith Wigglesworth preach, you will have to wait until you get to heaven to know what it was like, says W. Hacking. He goes on, I do not recollect ever hearing any other preacher quite like him. I had heard great preachers, eloquent preachers – both Pentecostal and non-Pentecostal as far as denomination is concerned – but Wigglesworth was out on his own.

He had no homiletics, but he certainly had dynamics. When I say dynamics, I do not mean that he was vociferous or boisterous. Actually, there was always poise, a reverence, and a dignity of demeanour in his presentation. Many of his sentences were abstract, often disconnected, sometimes enigmatical, sometimes even ungrammatical, but often pithy.

For example, he said,

> "Some like to read their bible in Hebrew. Some like to read their bible in Greek. I prefer to read mine in the Holy Ghost."

For the most part however, his sentences were filled with inspiration and revelation. The hearer was edified, inspired and changed. One sentence sometimes was like a sermon, capable of changing the course of your life. For example: *"Any man can be changed by faith,"* or *"Never say, 'I can't' if you are filled with the Holy Ghost."* The whole secret was that these were words from the lips of a man who was in close touch with God – a man on fire for God. #14

Polly is Dead

It was especially painful, when Wigglesworth's beloved wife died of heart failure. Smith and Polly were in their early fifties. Life was good. The business was very successful. The Mission was thriving with spiritual activity. Smith was now travelling to other cities and on this particular evening he had to leave for Glasgow, Scotland, for a preaching appointment, but he did not go. An event took place that was to change the whole course of his life. He *"lost"* the *"best girl in the world,"* as he called her. #15

Arriving at her deathbed, he commanded her to live, and she came back to life. However, as he held her in his arms, Polly told Wigglesworth that the Lord wanted to receive her and she wanted to go home. He kissed her and released her to heaven.

Wigglesworth lost his wife Polly in 1913, and two years later he was to receive yet another severe blow. His youngest son, George, died, this greatly puzzled him.

Loneliness added to the sorrow when he chose to remain single the rest of his thirty-four years. *"After [Polly's] funeral,"* he told a friend **eleven years later**, *"I went back and lay on her grave. I wanted to die there."* Wigglesworth said that God told him to leave the grave. *"I told him that if he would give me a double portion of the Spirit - my wife's and my own - I would go and preach the gospel."*

God answered the plumber's prayer, but Wigglesworth added that he sailed the seas alone and often wept because of his loneliness. #16

Blessed are they that Mourn

However, while preaching on the *"beatitudes"* some years later, Wigglesworth gave this personal account of what happened: *Blessed are the poor in spirit: for theirs is the Kingdom of heaven.* This is one of the richest places into which Jesus brings us.

The poor have a right to everything in heaven. *Theirs is.* Dare you believe it? Yes. I dare. I believe, I know, that I was very poor. When God's Spirit comes in as the ruling, controlling power of the life, he gives us God's revelation of our inward poverty. Showing us that God has come with one purpose, to bring heaven's best to earth, and that with Jesus he will indeed, *freely give us all things.*

An old man and an old woman had lived together for seventy years. Someone said to them, *You must have seen many clouds during those days.* They replied, *Where do the showers come from?* **You never get showers without clouds.** It is only the Holy Spirit who can bring us to the place of realisation of our poverty; but every time He does it, He opens the windows of heaven and the showers of blessing fall.

But I must recognise the difference between my own spirit and the Holy Spirit. My own spirit can do certain things on natural lines, can even weep and pray and worship, but it is all on a human plane. And we must not depend on our own human thoughts and activities or on our own personality.

If the baptism *[in the Holy Spirit]* means anything to you, it should bring you to the death of the ordinary, where you are no longer putting faith in your own understanding; but, conscious of your own poverty, you are ever yielded to the Spirit. Then it is that your body becomes filled with heaven on earth.

"Blessed are they that mourn: for they shall be comforted."

People get a wrong idea of mourning. Over in Switzerland they have a day set apart to take wreaths to graves. I laughed at the people's ignorance and said, *Why are you spending time around the graves? The people you love are not there. All that taking of flowers to the graves is not faith at all.* Those who died in Christ are gone to be with Him, which, Paul said, *is far better.*

My wife once said to me, *Smith, you watch me when I'm preaching. I get so near to heaven when I'm preaching that some day I'll be off.*

One night she was preaching and when she had finished, off she went. I was going to Glasgow and had said goodbye to her before she went to the meeting. As I was leaving the house, the doctor and policeman met me at the door. I knew she had got what she wanted. I could not weep, but I was in tongues, praising the Lord. On natural lines she was everything to me; but I could not mourn on natural lines, but just laughed in the Spirit.

The house was soon filled with People

The doctor said, *She is dead, and we can do no more for her.* I went up to her lifeless corpse and commanded death to give her up, and she came back to me for a moment. Then God said to me, *She is mine; her work is done.* I knew what He meant.

They laid her in the coffin. And I brought my sons and my daughter into the room and said, *Is she there?* They said, *No father.* I said, *We will cover her up.*

If you go mourning the loss of loved ones who have gone to be with Christ, I say it in love to you, you have never had the revelation of what Paul spoke of when he shows us that it is better to go than to stay. We read this in scripture. But the trouble is that people will not believe it. When you believe God, you will say, *Whatever it is, it is all right. If you want to take the one I love, it is all right Lord.*

Faith removes all tears of Self-Pity

Throughout this experience Smith's faith remained unshaken, and some of his associates reckoned that a new depth in his ministry became evident. #17

From that time, Wigglesworth's ministry had a remarkable power. He was single-minded in the Lord's work. He visited America and stunned audiences with his sense of God's grace and love. Wigglesworth was embraced by Pentecostals in the United States and quickly became the nation's most favoured evangelist. He travelled across the many continents, many times accompanied by his daughter Alice.

Wigglesworth laid hands on the sick and welcomed challenges, which would demonstrate how easy the impossible was for God. In Sweden, where police forbade him to lay on hands, he told those in the massive crowds to lay their hands upon themselves and know that they would be healed, and hundreds were.

Wigglesworth continued preaching well into his eighties. On March 12, 1947, just short of his eighty-eighth birthday, Wigglesworth achieved that home for which he had so longed. He had brought together believers of all faiths, and believers of all faiths rejoiced in knowing that he had attained the absolute communion, which he so dearly prized.

...Praise God

PART TWO

MISSIONARIES
TAKE PENTECOSTAL POWER

References

1) Sumrall, Lester. Pioneers of Faith. Copyright 1995. Published by Harrison House Inc. Printed in Tulsa Oklahoma, USA. p25-27

2) Pioneers of Faith. p112

3) Pioneers of Faith. p28

4) Pioneers of Faith. p29-32

5) Pioneers of Faith. p81-83

6) Liardon, Roberts. God's Generals. Copyright 1996. Published by Albury Publishing. Printed in Tulsa Oklahoma, USA. p43

7) Whittaker, Colin. Great Revivals. Copyright 1984. Published by Marshall Pickering. Printed in London. p144

8) Great Revivals. p102

9) Great Revivals. p102-104

10) Great Revivals. p99

11) Great Revivals. p99

12) Dixon, Patrick. Signs of Revival. Copyright 1995. Published by Kingsway Publications. Printed in Eastbourne, UK. p172

13) Hywel-Davies, Jack. Baptised by Fire, The Story of Smith Wigglesworth. Copyright 1987. Published by Hodder and Stoughton Limited. Printed in Kent, UK. p66-72

14) Hocking, W. Smith Wigglesworth Remembered. Copyright 1981. Published by Harrison House Inc. Printed in Tulsa Oklahoma, USA. p73

15)   Baptised by Fire, The Story of Smith Wigglesworth. p91

16)   Warren, Wayne, ed.   The Anointing of His Spirit, Smith Wigglesworth. Copyright 1994. Published by Servant Publications. Printed in Ann Arbor Michigan, USA. p19

17)   Baptised by Fire, The Story of Smith Wigglesworth. p91-92

❖
Ministry Profile

Doctor Alan Pateman, an apostle, is the President and Founder of **"Alan Pateman Ministries International"** (APMI), which was established in England back in 1987, a Christian-based *(parachurch)* non-profit and non-denominational outreach. This ministry is now focusing in two main areas: First **"Connecting for Excellence"** Apostolic Networking (CFE) and secondly, the teaching arm, **"LifeStyle International Christian University"** (LICU).

CFE is a multi-facetted missions organisation with the purpose of connecting leaders for divine opportunities and building lasting relationships, to touch the lives of leaders literally the world over. Apostle Dr Alan Pateman has to date ordained more than 500 ministers in over 50 NATIONS. In addition there are ministries, churches and schools who are in Association or Affiliation, looking to him for apostolic counsel and oversight.

Secondly LICU, which was founded in 2007, is a study program to help people discover their purpose and destiny. A global network of university campuses and correspondence students, demonstrating the Supernatural Kingdom of God through Doctrinal, Apostolic and Prophetic Teaching. Dr Alan holds the position of President/CEO, Professor of Theology, Biblical Studies and Apostolic Ministry. LICU is exploding throughout Europe, Asia and Africa, enhancing the Body of Christ

Dr Alan has authored more than 35 books including numerous teaching materials and LICU university courses (30) along with hundreds of Truth for the Journey articles on kingdom lifestyle *(that are regularly distributed globally via the internet).*

He is recognised as an Apostle, Bishop, Leadership Mentor, University Educator, Motivational Speaker, Connector and Author, who has also been featured on national and international TV and radio networks throughout the years.

Currently Apostle Alan, his wife Dr Jennifer reside in Lucca *(Tuscany)* Italy and travel out from their Apostolic Company.

- Alan Pateman Ph.D., D.Min., D.D., M.A., B.Th.

Academic Background

Dr. Alan Pateman attended several colleges throughout his training *(including studying Theology at Roffey Place, Horsham, UK and a Member of Kerygma - with Rev. Colin Urquhart and Dr. Bob Gordon - 1985-1987)* before being awarded a Doctorate of Divinity *(2006)* in recognition of his lifetime achievements by the International College of Excellence, now "DanEl Christian College" *(President: Dr. Robb Thompson USA)* also "Life Christian University" *(Dr. Douglas Wingate USA)* where he also earned a Bachelor of Theology B.Th. *(2006),* a Master of Arts in Theology M.A., a Doctor of Ministry in Theology D.Min., *(2007)* and Doctor of Philosophy in Theology Ph.D. *(2013)* from LICU.

❖

To Contact the Author

Please email:

Alan Pateman Ministries International

Email: apostledr@alanpateman.com
Web: www.AlanPatemanMinistries.com

*Please include your prayer requests
and comments when you write.*

❖

Other Books

Media, Spiritual Gateway

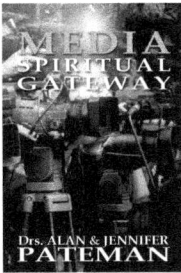

Let's face it; we live in the era of fake news! It's always existed, but never been quite so prominent. Today it's an all-out-war between fact and political fiction.

ISBN: 978-1-909132-54-2, Pages: 192,
Format: Paperback, Published: 2018
Also available in eBook format!

Millennial Myopia, From a Biblical Perspective

The standard for every generation is Jesus. However Millennial Myopia describes the trap of focusing everything on one particular generation or demographic cohort, at the exclusion and expense of all others. The Church cannot afford to make this mistake too.

ISBN: 978-1-909132-67-2, Pages: 216,
Format: Paperback, Published: 2017
Also available in eBook format!

Truth for the Journey Books

TONGUES, Our Supernatural Prayer Language

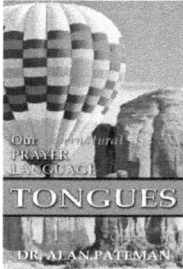

In writing to the church at Corinth, Paul encouraged them to continue the practice of speaking with other tongues in their worship of God and in their prayer lives as a means of spiritual edification. "He that speaketh in an unknown tongue edifies, charges, builds himself up like a battery."

ISBN: 978-1-909132-44-3, Pages: 144, Format: Paperback, Published: 2016
Also available in eBook format!

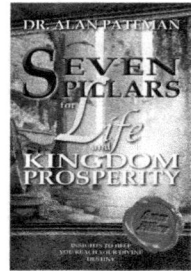

Seven Pillars for Life and Kingdom Prosperity

I submit these "Seven Pillars for Life and Kingdom Prosperity" to you, (Love, Prayer, Righteousness, Obedience, Connections, Management, Money). It's my desire that you walk in the triumphs that God has ordained for you.

ISBN: 978-1-909132-46-7, Pages: 220, Format: Paperback, Published: 2016
Also available in eBook format!

Seduction & Control: Infiltrating Society & the Church

This book is a glance into the world of seduction and control, how they try to influence the Church through many powerful avenues such as the New Age, sexual education in our schools, basic entertainment; things that touch our everyday lives in order that we effectively and gradually become desensitised.

ISBN: 978-1-909132-00-9, Pages: 156 Format: Paperback, Published: 2015
Also available in eBook format!

Truth for the Journey Books

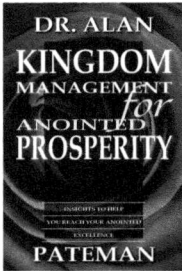

Kingdom Management for Anointed Prosperity

In his book, "Kingdom Management for Anointed Prosperity," Dr. Alan Pateman reveals how we can avoid living in continual crisis due to mismanagement. Life happens to all of us, but how we handle it matters most.

ISBN: 978-1-909132-34-4, Pages: 144, Format: Paperback, Published: 2015
Also available in eBook format!

Why War: A Biblical Approach to the Armour of God and Spiritual Warfare

Spiritual warfare means different things to different people, but from a biblical standpoint Ephesians 6:10-18 gives us the best biblical definition of spiritual warfare possible. We can also see how God has thoroughly equipped us for victory not just self defence!

ISBN: 978-1-909132-39-9, Pages: 180, Format: Paperback, Published: 2013
Also available in eBook format!

Forgiveness, The Key to Revival

Scripture is absolute when it comes to forgiveness. IF we forgive, THEN we are forgiven. It's that simple but no one said it was easy! Nonetheless, forgiveness can be likened to a spiritual key that unlocks spiritual doors and opportunities!

ISBN: 978-1-909132-41-2, Pages: 124, Format: Paperback, Published: 2013
Also available in eBook format!

The Early Years - Anointed Generals Past & Present (Part One of Four)

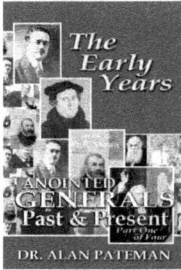

I pray that the divine anointing that is and has been upon these *Anointed Generals Past and Present* will be afforded to flow upon our heads, that those who are reported to be the generals of today would be strong enough - humble enough - to give time to those who desire to learn and grow and be established. So that what God has given to them will be our inheritance for the future.

ISBN: 978-1-909132-32-0, Pages: 132,
Format: Paperback, Published: 2012
Also available in eBook format!

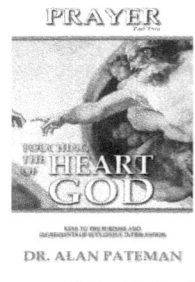

Prayer, Touching the Heart of God (Part Two)

Touching the Heart of God is the very essence of prayer. Whether we are petitioning God with very specific requests or consecrating ourselves before Him and rededicating our lives - whatever the case may be – the true essence of all praying is "Touching the Heart of God."

ISBN: 978-1-909132-12-2, Pages: 180,
Format: Paperback, Published: 2012
Also available in eBook format!

Prayer, Ingredients for Successful Intercession (Part One)

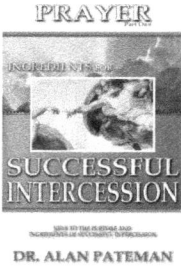

This Book is the first of two books on Prayer. Dr. Pateman provides an exhaustive study, showcasing the vital ingredients necessary for all successful prayer. An excellent power-packed teaching tool, either for the individual or for the local church prayer group, that's eager to lay a solid foundation but don't know where to start!

ISBN: 978-1-909132-11-5, Pages: 140,
Format: Paperback, Published: 2012
Also available in eBook format!

Truth for the Journey Books

Apostles: Can the Church Survive Without Them?

Before Jesus returns a significant increase of the anointing will be poured out on the Body of Christ, but can the Church handle such an anointing? *(Acts 5:5)* Billy Brim once said, "As much as the anointing is powerful to create, it is as powerfully destructive of evil." The fear of God will be restored with the apostolic and people will begin walking with such anointing, as we have never seen before!

ISBN: 978-1-909132-04-7, Pages: 164,
Format: Paperback, Published: 2012
Also available in eBook format!

Sexual Madness: In a Sexually Confused World

This book discusses the sensitive subject of political correctness in our world today and the growing fear of causing offence in the public arena. It also discusses the rise of homosexuality, pedophilia and all other forms of sexuality, as there are many. Including modern statistics on pornography.

ISBN: 978-1-909132-02-3, Pages: 160,
Format: Paperback, Published: 2012
Also available in eBook format!

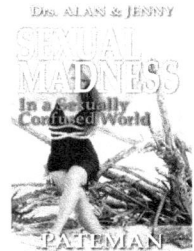

His Life is in the Blood

Blood is the trophy of every battle. The spilt blood of Jesus Christ is our trophy. It is our freedom from sin and bondage. Nothing can enter the blood-bought temples of the Holy Ghost! This book will encourage you to apply the blood of Jesus our Passover Lamb to your life, just as the children of Israel did in the Old Testament. Not merely talking or reading about it, but applying it.

ISBN: 978-1-909132-06-1, Pages: 152,
Format: Paperback, First Published: 2007
Also available in eBook format!

LIFESTYLE UNIVERSITY

Raising Up
Christian Leaders

Dear Friends,

Have you considered becoming one of our international students? We are privileged to welcome you, from around the world, to "LifeStyle International Christian University" *(the teaching arm of Alan Pateman Ministries International).* **An English speaking university** dedicated to your success; to see you trained and equipped to fully succeed in your God given Destiny.

It is our passion to raise up the leaders of tomorrow, who will have influence in all realms of authority, including the Body of Christ. Men and women of strategy, wisdom and true godliness, who'll stand with stature and maturity in this hour.

It's undeniable that in today's world, recognised education has become indispensable, therefore it is our desire to offer well balanced and well structured courses. Those that have been written by gifted and talented ministers of God, who seek to be inspired by God's Holy Spirit.

Consequently we have put together a **flexible curriculum,** designed both for correspondence students and campuses, which is a strategy to reach the distant learner; whether provincial, national or international. In fact we have many correspondence students from around the world, including a growing number of successful campuses, in various countries.

This is a growing platform, where men and women of dignity and passion, can grow and be established in their God given endeavours. As God is the healer of the nations, we pray and believe that many of our alumni will go on to **become world changers** in their own right.

We are proud of each and every one of our LICU students.
It would be our pleasure if you would join them on this incredible journey!

Doctor Alan Pateman

Alan Pateman Prof. Ph.D., D.Min., D.D., M.A., B.Th.
PRESIDENT AND CEO
www.licuuniversity.com   www.cfeapostolicnetwork.com
Email: info@licuuniversity.com   Mob: +39 366 329 1315

For more information visit our website/facebook or contact our office, using the details below:

Website: www.licuuniversity.com
Facebook: www.facebook.com/LICUMainCampus
Email: info@licuuniversity.com
Telephone: +39 366 329 1315

Alan Pateman Ministries
Presents

Conference

CONNECTING FOR
EXCELLENCE Lucca Italy

An international apostolic
and prophetic network

YOUR HOSTS: ALAN PATEMAN   JENNIFER PATEMAN

Please contact our office or download the registration form.
Registration fee: €40

apostledr@alanpateman.com, Tel. 0039 366 329 1315

WWW.ALANPATEMANMINISTRIES.COM

ALAN PATEMAN MINISTRIES
PRESENTS

TEACHING - LEARNING - LIVING
A MASTER CLASS
with Dr Alan Pateman

DR. ALAN IS AVAILABLE
TO HOLD TEACHING
SEMINARS ON SATURDAYS
WITH YOUR LEADERS /
MEMBERS AND THEN
MINISTER AT YOUR
SUNDAY SERVICE.
PLEASE CONTACT OUR
OFFICE FOR AVAILABILITY.

OFFICE: VIA DEL GALLO, 18,
55100 LUCCA (LU), ITALY
TEL. 0039 366 329 1315
APOSTLEDR@ALANPATEMAN.COM

www.alanpatemanministries.com

All Books Available

APMI PUBLICATIONS

Email: publications@alanpateman.com
*Also Available from Amazon.com
and other retail outlets.*

If you purchased this book through Amazon.com or other and enjoyed reading it, or perhaps one of my other books, I would be grateful if you could take a couple of minutes to write a Customer Review, many thanks.

www.ingramcontent.com/pod-product-compliance
Lightning Source LLC
Chambersburg PA
CBHW071452070426
42452CB00039B/1142